RENOUNCING EVERYTHING

RENOUNCING EVERYTHING

MONEY *and* DISCIPLESHIP *in* LUKE

Christopher M. Hays

Paulist Press
New York / Mahwah, NJ

Unless otherwise stated, the Scripture quotations contained herein are from the New Revised Standard Version: Catholic Edition, Copyright © 1989 and 1993, by the Division of Christian Education of the National Council of the Churches of Christ in the United States of America. Used by permission. All rights reserved.

Cover image: Caravaggio, photo courtesy of Wikimedia Commons
Cover design by Sharyn Banks
Book design by Lynn Else

Copyright © 2016 by Centre for Enterprise, Markets and Ethics

All rights reserved. No part of this publication may be reproduced, stored in a retrieval system, or transmitted in any form or by any means, electronic, mechanical, photocopying, recording, scanning, or otherwise, except as permitted under Section 107 or 108 of the 1976 United States Copyright Act, without the prior written permission of the Publisher. Requests to the Publisher for permission should be addressed to the Permissions Department, Paulist Press, 997 Macarthur Boulevard, Mahwah, NJ 07430, (201) 825-7300, fax (201) 825-8345, or online at www.paulistpress.com.

Library of Congress Cataloging-in-Publication Data

Names: Hays, Christopher M., 1983– author.
Title: Renouncing everything : money and discipleship in Luke / Christopher M. Hays.
Description: New York : Paulist Press, 2016. | Includes bibliographical references and index.
Identifiers: LCCN 2016022376 (print) | LCCN 2016032460 (ebook) | ISBN 9780809149919 (pbk. : alk. paper) | ISBN 9781587686184 (Ebook)
Subjects: LCSH: Wealth—Biblical teaching. | Money—Biblical teaching. | Bible. Luke—Criticism, interpretation, etc. | Bible. Acts—Criticism, interpretation, etc.
Classification: LCC BS2545.W37 H39 2016 (print) | LCC BS2545.W37 (ebook) | DDC 226.4/06—dc23
LC record available at https://lccn.loc.gov/2016022376

ISBN 978-0-8091-4991-9 (paperback)
ISBN 978-1-58768-618-4 (e-book)

Published by Paulist Press
997 Macarthur Boulevard
Mahwah, New Jersey 07430

www.paulistpress.com

Printed and bound in the
United States of America

Dedicated to the Lord Griffiths of Fforestfach

Contents

Foreword *by Thomas J. Massaro, SJ* ix

Preface xv

Acknowledgments xvii

Abbreviations xix

Chapter 1: The Problems 1

Chapter 2: Toward an Explanation 15

Chapter 3: Total Commitment to God 25

Chapter 4: Models of Discipleship in Luke 35

Chapter 5: Models of Discipleship in Acts 53

Chapter 6: Why Renounce All? 67

Chapter 7: Guidance for the Contemporary Disciple 81

Notes 97

Bibliography 109

Index of Sources 113

Foreword

"WHAT ARE YOU GOING TO DO with that money?" The first time I faced that challenging question was as a small child, when a kindly uncle slipped a five-dollar bill into the envelope containing my annual birthday card. Whatever answer I muttered in reply probably reflected the same level of self-awareness I displayed upon the receipt of my regular allowance (generally measured in small coins, rarely actual dollar bills) for performing household chores. The ethical insight I mustered on that occasion took the form of a fumbling calculation along these lines: "Let's see…if I buy a ten-pack of my favorite candy bar today, maybe there will be enough left over to purchase another chocolate treat tomorrow." Oh for the simple days of youth!

The question of how to use wealth is a serious and complex one—both for those who explicitly and eagerly seek scriptural guidance and for those who would judge scripture irrelevant—if they even think of it at all. The example above may seem trivial, but in my life, the experience of a childhood plagued by the tension between possessing a sweet tooth, on the one hand, and tragically limited spending money, on the other hand, already raised some of the key dynamics governing wealth allocation in a world of limited resources. How may we justify present consumption of scarce goods in light of anticipated future needs and wants? What is the prudent course of action for the candy lover on a tight budget? If the younger version of me had been a bit more socially aware, a further tangle of questions would have arisen: How should I factor in the wants and needs of others as I planned my spending spree? Under what conditions are more serious claims upon my newfound wealth rightly considered relevant, even obligatory? While

RENOUNCING EVERYTHING

it is probably too much to expect from a young boy, a further line of inquiry would edge toward the spiritual, touching on the often inconvenient demands of discipleship. Might God be calling me to renounce some of my windfall to engage in—employing an old-fashioned phrase here—a bit of self-mortification? There always seemed to be bottomless complications to ponder, when all I wanted to do was to savor the delicious possibilities presented by this novel type of birthday present. A five-dollar bill had suddenly morphed into the Apple of Discord, or Pandora's Box, or ... (insert here your preferred morally problematic mythological object).

In the grand scheme of things, it is a nice problem to have, this question of how to dispose of surplus wealth. A glance at the historical record places the matter into revealing perspective. For most of human history, hardly anyone had to worry about such questions. From prehistoric times, through ancient, medieval, and even modern times—indeed, right up to the birth of our mass consumption society mere decades ago—with so few resources to go around, the best an individual, family, or tribe could do would be to preserve the leftovers of a harvest or hunt to ward off the threat of the next winter, drought, or famine. The development of increasingly sophisticated monetary and banking systems along the march of human history provided the convenience of storing value and offered new opportunities for commerce and investment. However, engaging in high finance was beyond the reach of practically everyone except royalty and nobility. Even today, in an era of unprecedented wealth and ostentatious consumption available to the elite, only a small minority of the residents of this world have risen very far above the level of sheer material subsistence. Most inhabitants of our world continue the practice of living paycheck to paycheck—if they can find employment at all. When there is little or nothing to spare, the grand questions of philanthropy, social obligation, and even voluntary renunciation of wealth are hardly on the front burner. To cite a phrase common in contemporary parlance, "That is a very First-World problem."

When people of conscience do acquire something to spare, they naturally seek out wisdom to guide the allocative decisions they face. Among the key sources of wisdom are the texts of religious traditions. For people who revere the Bible, the Scriptures

Foreword

are (at least at first glance) a treasure trove of advice and counsel regarding the proper use of material goods. Many parts of the Bible contain promising material for this purpose, for the books of the Hebrew and Christian Scriptures provide a portrayal of the universe, of its Creator, and of us mortal beings that orients us to the true purpose of our lives and calls us beyond ourselves. If God indeed created each material thing with some purpose, then maybe the Holy Scriptures will reveal these secrets. The astute observer of biblical materials will quickly discover deep tensions, even contradictions, in how parts of the Bible treat the reality of wealth and its use. We would, in the end, search in vain for a single "biblical approach to possessions."

All caveats and disclaimers notwithstanding, the Gospel of Luke emerges as one particularly promising location to discover the obligations that people of faith might experience regarding possessions and wealth. Along with its companion narrative, Acts of the Apostles, Luke's Gospel contains an extraordinarily large amount of material on the topic of ethical living *in general*, and the obligations of disciples to dispose properly of their belongings *in particular*. All of us aspiring followers of Jesus are well served to examine in detail what the New Testament relates, in the shorter sayings as well as longer parables and narratives of Jesus, about the responsible use of wealth. Despite the dizzying complexities of the subject matter, the reader of this present volume will come away with a rather comprehensive picture of what Luke's Jesus says and does regarding these important duties.

In the first chapter of this book, Christopher Hays asks the question: "So what do we do with Luke's wealth ethics?" Neither Hays's field of biblical scholarship nor my own field of Christian social ethics has yet come up with a firm answer. Both interpreters of scripture and theorists of Christian morality have recognized the twin puzzles Hays describes in his first chapter: the inconsistency and impracticality of the claims in Luke's Gospel regarding riches and possessions. If we can get past the maddening leaps of logic in the teachings of Jesus in Luke's Gospel, certain sturdy truths and paths of understanding do emerge. But of course, discerning socially responsible courses of action is always more of an art than a science, and determining a fitting response to the ethical challenges contained in the Gospel of Luke is an ongoing task. The persistence of disagreements about the demands of gospel morality is to be expected; indeed, the existence of differences of biblical interpretation is a sign of vitality in any community of sincere belief. Uniformity of belief and rigidity of practice, even if they could ever be achieved among collectivities of fallible humans, would in the end prove stifling. Our religious creeds and dogmas serve us well when they inspire us to grow in faith and stretch our current understandings of our ethical duties, but they fail us when they bind us in a straightjacket of unthinking compliance with rules and norms we passively receive but never scrutinize. The healthiest variety of faith is one that provides us with meaning and identity, yet is still open-ended enough that we feel the challenge to try on new moral equipment and explore new territory.

This book does well to consider both the supply side (questions facing those with wealth to dispose of) and the demand side (the desperate needs of our struggling world). Indeed, in the very teachings of Jesus, poverty and wealth are linked in unmistakable ways. The dramatic parable of the Rich Man (Dives) and Lazarus the Beggar (see Luke 16:19–31) is just one of many places where Jesus juxtaposes the plight of the wretched and the luxury of the affluent, offering the strongest of moral lessons with the highest of stakes. If we are ever to address the topic of economic justice in an adequate way—one true to the social solidarity that Christian faith must include—both sides of the economic equation must be taken seriously and connected prudently. Constructive ethical reflection on the demands of Christian discipleship will always hold together the paired realities of surplus wealth and dire need. After all, the affluent and the desperately poor share a common life on a shared planet, however easy it may be at times to forget this fundamental fact of human existence. The vast distances we create through segregation, both social and geographical, are in the end artificial and open to remedial efforts. Through creative responses to human need, from simple interpersonal generosity to massive social movements to enact human solidarity, we retain the ability to bridge the divides and overcome the chasm between rich and poor in our world. As something of a bonus, the final pages of this book offer a most welcome intimate glimpse at the author's own experience of walking the path of renunciation; this felicitous foray into humble self-revelation gently invites all readers to take

Foreword

the next good step toward self-awareness regarding detachment from riches and "the principle of enough."

Like all perceptive writings on religious ethics, this book will prompt more questions among readers than it can possibly answer in a definitive way. Both for Luke in his time and for us in our time, it is tantalizing to ponder these and related lines of inquiry: What level of almsgiving is required? Do some people receive a pass, or a partial relaxation of the most austere demands? Am I justified in keeping anything for myself at all? If so, what principles should guide my economic decisions? While these questions will surely remain with readers long after they put down this volume, every chapter between the covers of this book supplies an account that will contribute to richer understanding of this crucial topic.

Renouncing Everything is a most welcome volume that provides great service to the Christian community. While each reader will surely discover his or her own favorite contributions, let me venture to identify two core accomplishments. First, it provides an eminently reliable interpretation of the Lukan material on property, possessions, and their proper disposal. Second, it ventures some educated guesses regarding the meaning for our times of what we read in scripture. Whether you are a venture capitalist, a "trust fund baby," a blue-collar worker with bills to pay, or a kid with a birthday windfall of five cool bucks and a penchant for sweets, anyone with a conscience and a high regard for scripture can find in the pages that follow much insight into what the words of Luke's Gospel might mean for us today. In accomplishing these impressive objectives, this volume emerges as an outstanding model for responsible biblical interpretation fitted to the challenges of our times.

Thomas J. Massaro, SJ
Berkeley, California
June 2016

Preface

THIS VOLUME IS BASED on my doctoral thesis, which was originally published as *Luke's Wealth Ethics: A Study in Their Coherence and Character*, Wissenschaftliche Untersuchungen zum Neuen Testament II, vol. 275 (Tübingen: Mohr Siebeck, 2010). That book, however, was aimed at scholars, not at students or laypersons. So I welcomed the opportunity to write a version of the book for this latter audience.

The present book is only a fourth in length of *Luke's Wealth Ethics* and not nearly as dense as that academic monograph. In addition, this book is written with an explicitly Christian stance, such that I ask both the scholarly and the practical questions that arise from the belief that Luke and Acts are not just interesting historical artifacts, but Scripture.

Obviously, a short, popular book cannot answer even a fraction of the academic questions that a study like this might generate, so the reader with additional inquires is encouraged to read the expanded treatment available in *Luke's Wealth Ethics* and the content of chapter 7 in a forthcoming article to be published in *Evangelical Quarterly*. While I do not generally footnote the relevant pages of *Luke's Wealth Ethics*, since self-citation is a tiresome affair (probably more so for the reader than the author), on the occasions when I do refer explicitly to this volume, I merely use the abbreviation *LWE*.

Acknowledgments

THE PRODUCTION OF THIS BOOK was made possible by the generous support of the Centre for Enterprise, Markets and Ethics (CEME). I was first approached about becoming linked to the CEME in 2012, when Dr. Richard Turnbull, the director of the newly minted think tank, dropped me a line as I was wrapping up my British Academy Postdoctoral Fellowship at Keble College in the University of Oxford. Dr. Turnbull explained to me that the CEME was being formed to examine how Judeo-Christian ethics might support the flourishing of a more moral form of market capitalism. Richard articulated to me that the Chairman of the Board of the CEME, Brian Griffiths (Lord Griffiths of Fforestfach), had read my recently published doctoral thesis[1] and the two of them thought I might be a good fit for the think tank.

I admit to feeling skeptical of Richard's claim that Lord Griffiths had read my book *and* liked it, not only because of the imposter syndrome from which all young academics suffer, but also because Lord Griffiths wrote *The Creation of Wealth: A Christian's Case for Capitalism* (Downers Grove, IL: Intervarsity, 1984), which was one of the first works on wealth ethics I studied when, as a master's student, I began to research issues of poverty and economics. Lord Griffiths has been, *inter multa alia*, Professor of Banking and Finance at the London School of Economics, Director of the Bank of England, and the Head of Margaret Thatcher's Policy Unit.

Upon the occasion of meeting in person, taking coffee in the Senior Common Room of Keble College, I found that Lord Griffiths (or Brian, as he graciously insisted that I call him), had indeed read my book with care, and that he *still* liked it. In fact, it was at that first coffee in Keble that Brian encouraged me to write a small, popular version of my doctoral thesis. Indeed, as I was made a Fellow of the CEME, Brian and Richard kindly commissioned that popularization of the thesis, which became the present book. For their encouragement and financial support of this project, I am exceedingly grateful.

Several months later, Christopher Frechette from Paulist Press reached out with a similar idea, and the CEME thought Paulist would be a good fit for the book, for which I am very appreciative. I am also thankful to Mohr Siebeck, the publisher of *Luke's Wealth Ethics*, for happily assenting to this popularization of the monograph for a broader audience.

I am thankful to my wonderful wife, Michelle, who reprised her role as the editor of *Luke's Wealth Ethics* and applied her red ink to this volume, with much patience. I am also indebted to Syman and Mary Catherine Stevens and the Trinity Forum Academy; in order to help me finish this book, they invited me to Osprey Point for a writing retreat, offering me a cottage and a week in a cozy, oak-paneled library overlooking the Chesapeake Bay.

This book is dedicated to Lord Griffiths, and not exclusively because of the CEME's essential part in bringing about the publication. Lord Griffiths and his lovely wife, Rachel, have sponsored not only my academic research but also my vocation as a missionary in South America. Brian's enthusiasm for my work and his desire to see me flourish as an academic even after leaving Oxford have been greater kindnesses to me than I can adequately express. For all those things, I am profoundly grateful.

Abbreviations

1En.	*First Enoch*
1QS	Rule of the Community
4Q171	Psalms Pesher[a]
4Q427	Hodayot[a]
Abr.	*De Abrahamo*
Aem.	*Aemilius Paullus*
Ages.	*Agesilaus*
A.J.	*Antiquitates judaicae*
b.	Babylonian Talmud
Ben.	*De beneficiis*
Ber.	*Berakot*
B.J.	*Bellum judaicum*
CD	Damascus Document
Cleom.	*Cleomenes*
Demetr.	*Demetrius*
Demon.	*Demonax*
Dig.	*Digesta*
Ep.	*Epistle*
Eth. nic.	*Ethica nichomachea*
Evag.	*Evagoras* (Oration 9)
Herm.	Shepherd of Hermas
Hist. eccl.	*Historia ecclesiastica*
Leg.	*Leges*

LWE	*Luke's Wealth Ethics: A Study in Their Coherence and Character*, Wissenschaftliche Untersuchungen zum Neuen Testament II, vol. 275 (Tübingen: Mohr Siebeck, 2010).
m.	Mishnah
Migr.	*De migratione Abrahami*
Mor.	*Moralia*
Neof.	*Neofiti*
Off.	*De officiis*
Onq.	*Onkelos*
Per.	*Pericles*
P.Oxy.	Oxyrhynchus papyrus
Pol.	*Politica*
Prob.	*Quod omnis probus liber sit*
Ps.-Jon.	*Pseudo-Jonathan*
Resp.	*Respublica*
Sib. Or.	*Sibylline Oracles*
Sim.	*Similitude*
T.Jud.	*Testament of Judah*
Tg.	*Targum*
Tim.	*Timaeus*
Vita Pyth.	*De vita pythagorica*

CHAPTER 1

The Problems

THINGS ARE DESPERATELY WRONG. That's not really a point of contention. Poverty drives boys to steal, youths to kill, and girls to sell what should never be bought. Hunger plagues hundreds of millions around the world; the numbers are so large that they lose all meaning as it becomes difficult to imagine nations of undernourished people. In the United States, the street corners are haunted by hollow-eyed, bearded veterans; cramped motels shelter families whose homes have been repossessed. The 2008 financial crisis is in our rearview mirror, but we have not fixed the system that fostered predatory lending, credit default swaps, and mortgage-backed securities. We wait for the other shoe to drop.

We are often overwhelmed by the suffering, the fear, the need to assign blame, and the urgency to find an answer. Perhaps we hurry to Facebook to vent our righteous indignation, all the while knowing this response does not solve anything. We want desperately to find a fixed point on the horizon, a North Star to help orient us amidst the cacophonous voices of the media such as CNN and *Forbes* magazine, and social media.

Some may wonder if Jesus can do that for us. After all, Jesus has a way of cutting through the noise. Jesus does a lot of "straight talking" about poverty and riches, especially in Luke's Gospel. He tells us that the poor are blessed (Luke 6:20) and that the rich are in trouble (Luke 6:24). He tells us that if we follow him and don't look back (Luke 9:62), if we feed the hungry (Luke 14:13–34) and give alms to the poor (Luke 12:33), then we will have treasures in heaven (Luke 12:34). And so we wonder if this straight-talking

1

Jesus can help us do an end-run around the pundits and the talking heads and finally give us the peace of mind in knowing that we are doing the right thing.

Luke's Gospel does tell us a great deal about how God wants his people to use their possessions in a world of injustice. But as any reader of the Gospels knows, when you go to Jesus for answers, you may not like the answers you receive.

LUKE'S WEALTH ETHICS

Luke writes extensively about morality and money, about how we should think of poverty, and what we should do with our possessions, what we might call "wealth ethics." But Luke's wealth ethics are notoriously tricky and a close examination of his many teachings on money uncovers two problems:

1. Luke seems to contradict himself. (Inconsistency)
2. Luke seems absurdly unrealistic. (Impracticality)

LUKE'S INCONSISTENCY

As noted earlier, some people who feel the weight of twenty-first-century inequality and injustice seek answers in the Bible. But what happens when those answers are less than systematic? What happens when even Luke, the biblical author who is arguably the most interested in money, can't seem to get his story straight? As one Lukan scholar explains, the problem with Luke's writing seems to be that "although Luke consistently talks about possessions, he does not talk about possessions consistently."[1]

Consider the tensions between the following texts. Sometimes, Luke's Jesus[2] encourages people to give alms (Luke 11:41; cf. Acts 9:36; 10:2). On the surface, this may seem straightforward, but then the question of *how much* one should give arises. Today, we may think of almsgiving in terms of loose change, or five dollars if one is feeling particularly generous, but Luke's Jesus says that his followers should *"sell your possessions*, and give alms" (Luke 12:33, emphasis mine).

How many possessions should one sell to give alms? A tunic? A set of tools? Earthenware bowls? The family donkey? Jesus doesn't pull any punches. He tells one rich man, "Sell all that you own and distribute the money to the poor" (Luke 18:22), and when the gentleman looks crestfallen, Jesus clarifies that failing to do as he was commanded means that the man will not be able to enter the kingdom of God (18:23–24), that is, he won't "inherit eternal life" (18:18). However harsh that may seem, it fits naturally with Jesus' categorical statement: "Any one of you who does not renounce all of his possessions cannot be my disciple" (14:33, my translation). Likewise, Jesus says, "Blessed are you who are poor, for yours is the kingdom of God" (6:20). In that light, literal self-impoverishment might not be a bad idea, if indeed it is a prerequisite for inclusion in the kingdom.

Consequently, Jesus calls for serious divestiture for the purpose of almsgiving. Indeed, he tells people that they have to renounce all of their possessions if they want to follow him. That creates obvious *practical* questions, but from an exegetical perspective (i.e., just understanding what Luke is saying), the imperative to renounce all possessions is not a problem in its own right; it is perfectly plausible that an ancient author would say something that a contemporary reader finds unpalatable. The *exegetical problem* arises when one goes on to read in Luke's Gospel about all the people who don't divest themselves and nonetheless also don't incur Jesus' censure, even though Jesus clearly said that his disciples have to renounce all their possessions.

For example, when Jesus sends his disciples out to preach that the kingdom of God has come near (10:1–11), he tells them not to bring any money or even a bag in which to carry food (10:4). They won't need supplies, he explains, because they can expect to be sheltered and fed by the people to whom they preach (10:5–9). This then raises the question: If the disciples are preaching Jesus' message in the villages, shouldn't the villagers also give up their homes and possessions in response to that message? But then where would the disciples stay? Then who would feed the disciples? They'd be veritably sawing off the branch on which they sat!

RENOUNCING EVERYTHING

Nonetheless, contrary to what one might infer, the disciples do not seem to have told people to give up their possessions. Rather, Jesus told them to bless the house in which they lodged (10:5) and to cure the sick people there (10:9), which seems to indicate rather strongly that it is legitimate for the disciples' audiences *not* to give up their possessions. In fact, when one flips over to Luke's second book, the Acts of the Apostles, there are several people with houses who seem to be depicted positively.[3] So does Luke think that it is OK to have homes and possessions, or not?

There are some texts in which the Gospel of Luke seems to strike a balance between divestiture and possession. For example, John the Baptist tells people with two cloaks to give up one, and to share their food with the poor (Luke 3:11). At first, this 50/50 split seems to be echoed in the example of Zacchaeus, who says that he will give half of his possessions to the poor (19:8). However, instead of saying, "You're halfway there!" (as one might expect if *complete* renunciation were a prerequisite to salvation), Jesus decisively exclaims, "Today salvation has come to this house" (19:9).

To complicate matters further, there are parts of Luke's writing that sound socialist. For example, Luke says that in the Jerusalem community, "no one claimed private ownership of any possessions, but everything they owned was held in common.... There was not a needy person among them, for as many as owned lands or houses sold them and brought the proceeds of what was sold" (Acts 4:32, 34).[4] This text is so striking that Karl Kautsky, the secretary of Friedrich Engels (the coauthor of *The Communist Manifesto*), argued that the Christian religion demanded communism, citing Acts as his evidence.[5]

Almsgiving or communism; divestiture or hospitality? Which of these does Luke really want his readers to adopt? One cannot very well sell one's house and then offer hospitality. *This* is the major exegetical problem in Luke's wealth ethics: he seems to contradict himself. A lot.

The Problems

LUKE'S IMPRACTICALITY

The second problem with Luke's wealth ethics is that some things he teaches seem undesirable, irresponsible, or impractical. This is not an exegetical problem per se—that is, it is not the sort of problem New Testament scholars typically address. The basic job of the New Testament scholar is just to describe what the biblical authors say in terms that are as accurate and objective as possible. They work hard not to let their religious commitments or cultural suppositions distort their reading of the first-century text. Consequently, New Testament exegesis should not care whether or not what Luke or Jesus thinks is "workable." Exegesis should simply clarify what Luke or Jesus seems to have said.

This effort to be objective is commendable.[6] After all, even a committed religious person who does not care at all for scholarship would still say that they want to know what Luke or Jesus "really" said, and scholarly objectivity aids this. Nonetheless, the reason that most people read the New Testament is not because they think that Luke is a literary artist on par with Euripides, that James is a philosopher of the same caliber as Seneca, or that Paul is as funny as Lucian. Rather, most people read the New Testament because they are religious and because they believe that the New Testament communicates truth about God, about God's interaction with the world, and about how humans should live.[7] Consequently, bracketing out the question of whether one can actually *do* what Jesus in Luke teaches seems tantamount to interrupting the conversation just as it gets interesting.

With that said, there are numerous reasons to think that Luke's wealth ethics are not very practical or desirable. After all, if you sell everything you have and give all the money to the poor, do you not then become a poor person in need of money? Does selling everything you have mean that you can still draw a paycheck? Is it coherent to demand that a disciple of Jesus must divest herself and then argue that she should be cared for by other people who do not divest themselves? Or—if one is inclined to take the socialist route—what is one to do about people who "sponge" off the community, who do not work as hard as they should, and who do not contribute to the common good? Is that sustainable as a long-term practice?

Less pious but likely more influential are the other considerations of whether or not people actually *want* to live the way that is presented in Luke's Gospel. Am I willing to give up all but one pair of clothes? Do I want to have a crowd of guests eating in my house every day? Or indeed, should I sell my house and then oblige my children to sleep on the street?

So what do we do with Luke's wealth ethics? If the actions he requires are utterly impractical, and if his apparently perpetual self-contradictions indicate that he hasn't thought things through very clearly, is it worth bothering with him? How do we deal with the fact that Luke and Acts are part of the canon and clearly very interested in wealth ethics, however much they may not be *good* at wealth ethics? In short, can Luke's wealth ethics be salvaged?

SOME EXPLANATIONS: STRENGTHS AND WEAKNESSES

Most scholars have thought so; the last century generated stacks of books and essays explaining Luke's teachings about wealth ethics. Some of those explanations seem attractive for practical reasons (i.e., they say things that sit well with our contemporary practice), but are less convincing exegetically. Others have much to offer both exegetically and practically, but may not quite satisfy all objections. In any scenario, before launching into our discussion of Luke's texts in detail, it is worth examining the interpretive options on the table.

Scholarly explanations of Luke's teachings on money and poverty fall into four basic categories, which might be called the *interim* explanation, the *literary* explanation, the *bi-vocational* explanation, and the *personalist* explanation. Let's briefly sketch the broad contours of each view and where the strengths and weakness lie.[8] In the course of this process, we will also highlight how each position bears on the subject of Luke's moral normativity (i.e., how people should act in light of Luke's teachings). This is not to imply that the scholars advocating each view came to their conclusions in order to achieve a particular "application"—that would be an insult to their objectivity. The intention is simply to indicate that certain interpretations do lend themselves more naturally to particular ethical conclusions or help the reader to avoid particular ethical conclusions.

The Interim Explanation

The basic argument of the interim explanation is that Jesus' superradical teachings on divestiture were not intended for all people in all times. Rather, when Jesus called people to renunciation of possessions, he only meant them to do so during the *interim* period of his earthly ministry, before he died, as the disciples journeyed with him toward Judea. After all, most of Jesus' statements on divestiture fall between 9:51 and 19:28 (the so-called Lukan travel narrative), as Jesus and the disciples walk from Galilee to Jerusalem, where Jesus would be crucified. The impending crucifixion of Jesus thus dominates the narrative and provides the framework in which to understand all the moral teachings therein. After all, just before Jesus' categorical statement on renunciation of possessions, he says, "Whoever does not carry the cross and follow me cannot be my disciple" (Luke 14:27). This is taken to imply that Jesus literally expects his disciples to die with him in Jerusalem.

In light of that unique and urgent situation (i.e., the crucifixion), the argument goes, the disciples of Jesus had to cast off material and familial ties, lest they draw back from dying faithfully with their Lord. After his death, people could resume the more traditional wealth ethics that one finds described in the Old Testament: attention to justice for the vulnerable, generous care for the poor, persistence of private property, and so on. But one could safely set aside the radical divestiture of possessions, as that was part of the unique situation surrounding Jesus' imminent death.

In its favor, this reading recognizes that Luke's ethics are part and parcel of the more fundamental task of following Jesus, a task that entails imitation of Jesus' self-sacrifice on behalf of his people. This interpretation also seems attractive because it lets the reader off the hook for the invasive and apparently illogical demands of complete renunciation; since the reader is not in the same historical situation as the first followers of Jesus, the reader need not adhere to Jesus' teachings to those first disciples.

There are, however, a number of problems with this explanation. In the first place, it is wrong to see Luke 14:27 as a mere command that the first disciples die with Jesus in Jerusalem. The first time Jesus invoked this particular theme was when he said, "If any want to become my followers, let them deny themselves and take up their cross daily and follow me" (Luke 9:23). While taking up the cross daily does not exclude the possibility of literal death for the sake of following Jesus, it is certainly the case that you cannot physically die each day; as such, the verse probably focuses on the necessity of suffering and sacrifice for Jesus' followers, many of whom, in spite of daily carrying their cross, would not die before they saw the kingdom of God (9:27). So we should not think that the commandment to bear one's cross was nullified after Jesus died. It is therefore problematic to claim that the accompanying commandment to renounce one's possessions also expired on the day Jesus was crucified.

Similarly, Luke's comments about poverty and renunciation are *not confined* to the period in which the disciples accompanied Jesus to Jerusalem. In the first place, the teaching in Luke 6:20 ("Blessed are you who are poor, for yours is the kingdom of God") does not take place during the travel narrative (Luke 9:51—19:28). Secondly, the renunciation of possessions by the disciples began well before the journey to Jerusalem; Peter, James, John, and Levi left everything behind to follow Jesus at the beginning of his Galilean ministry (cf. 5:11, 28). Likewise, the disciples continue to practice divestiture of possessions and property after Jesus' death and resurrection (Acts 4:34–37). If Jesus' wealth ethics were only intended for an interim period prior to his death, the Jerusalem Christians apparently didn't get the message.

Finally, the sheer amount of space that Luke dedicates to ethics in his travel narrative should ward us off the interim explanation. Luke spends a great deal more time talking about ethics than both Mark and John combined, and while the quantity of moral material in his Gospel is similar to that of Matthew, Luke shoehorns most of it into this ten-chapter travel narrative. It seems implausible that Luke would spend so much time elaborating his moral arguments[9] if he did not consider the morality prescribed therein to be incumbent upon his readers. For these reasons, few scholars have found the interim explanation to be a compelling account of Luke's teachings on money.

The Literary Explanation

Another way to account for the inconsistencies and impracticalities of Luke's wealth ethics is to ascribe some of the troubling verses to other *literary* sources. New Testament scholars often practice what is called "source criticism" or "literary criticism." Proceeding from the premise that the Synoptic authors utilized some earlier written sources in compiling their Gospels, biblical scholars try to identify what elements of the canonical Gospels came from earlier texts. In some more ambitious moments, scholars will also try to imagine what sort of a community might have been responsible for the source text in question. This is all relevant to the subject of Lukan wealth ethics because some scholars suggest that the inconsistencies in Luke's teachings derive from different source texts he used, sources whose teachings are actually incompatible with one another.

While the details of these literary explanations differ, their broad strokes are the same. Their advocates first argue that some of the particularly "radical" verses in Luke (i.e., the injunction to divestiture in 12:33, or the strong condemnations of the rich in 6:24 and 16:19–26) do not necessarily derive from Jesus himself, but instead were part of the teaching of a first-century group that was distinct from the Jesus-followers who later came to be the apostolic Church. (Sometimes the reconstructed group is identified with "Ebionites"[10] or "wandering charismatic radicals"[11] or the "itinerant Q-community.") At some point, the teachings of the more radical group were written down and circulated, and Luke utilized those writings, alongside others, in composing his own Gospel.

The argument entails that Luke himself had a more moderate wealth ethic, emphasizing generous almsgiving and hospitality. Nonetheless, Luke utilized the stark accounts of divestiture and grizzly condemnations of the rich in his source texts in order to critique the selfish affluent people in his own community (perhaps failing to realize that in so doing he introduced significant contradictions into the teachings he ascribed to Jesus). Thus, the inconsistencies in the wealth ethics of Luke are not reflective of inconsistencies in Jesus' own historical teachings or in Luke's own thought; they are rather supposed to be the consequences of including radical source texts within a more moderate moral framework. The implicit payoff of this reading is that the reader of Luke's Gospel need not feel obliged to believe the stark condemnation of the rich or to divest thoroughly, unless there is a felt need to identify with a long-extinct, nonapostolic sect.

Notwithstanding the initial plausibility of such a reconstruction, the literary explanations have not gained much traction in the broader academy. Some of this is due to the vulnerability of the historical communities supposedly "behind" Luke's source texts. Constructing a source text itself is a challenging endeavor (to say the least); using the details of that source text to imagine characteristics of *its* generating community only compounds speculation. It is true that in the 1970s and '80s—when literary explanations flourished—the identification of the source text with "Ebionites" or "wandering charismatics" or an itinerant "Q community" was considered more plausible. Since then, however, each of these reconstructions has fallen out of favor, for both source-critical and historical reasons.

Another vulnerability of literary explanations is their tendency to divorce the obtrusive elements of Luke's wealth ethics from Jesus himself. Historical Jesus scholarship now recognizes that Jesus himself was strongly critical of wealth, seeing it as a grave danger to spiritual fruitfulness (Matt 13:22; Mark 4:19; Luke 8:14) and indeed to one's inclusion in the kingdom of God (Matt 19:23–26; Mark 10:23–27; Luke 18:24–27). It is also undisputed that Jesus called for complete divestiture of possessions on at least one occasion (Matt 19:21; Mark 10:21; Luke 18:22).[12] Such scholarship makes it harder to set aside Luke's teachings on renunciation and relegating them to an idiosyncratic source text.

Finally, these literary explanations are difficult to square with the increasing consensus about the level of Luke's literary artistry. Since the late 1980s and early '90s, New Testament scholars have shifted from seeing Luke as a hapless cut-and-paste dilettante, recognizing instead that he, like the other Synoptic Evangelists, was quite a talented narrator. This is not to deny that Luke used sources, but reveals how problematic it is to surmise that Luke simply failed to recognize the major wealth-ethical inconsistencies between his source documents. Furthermore, it seems careless to argue that the acerbic source texts were introduced simply to threaten the rich, when Luke 14:33 categorically claims that *nobody* can be Jesus' disciple without renouncing all possessions. Therefore, however much Luke may have used sources in his work, it is not sufficient to brush off the unpalatable portions of his Gospel as being mere vestiges of his sources. At the very least, the basic thrust of the radical traditions derives from Jesus himself, and Luke thoroughly and positively integrates them into his Gospel.

The Bi-Vocational Explanation

Although the interim and the literary hypotheses do not present us with significant resources for addressing the problems associated with Lukan wealth ethics, the *bi-vocational* explanation has a good deal to commend it.

The basic premise of the bi-vocational explanation is that Luke distinguishes between two different groups of people who follow Jesus (e.g., disciples vs. crowds; the itinerant vs. the non-itinerant). It is argued that Jesus' teachings about renunciation and divestiture were aimed at those in (pardon the anachronism) "full-time ministry," like the apostles and evangelists. By contrast, other adherents of the Jesus movement are enjoined to more modest forms of generosity and hospitality.

This solution takes a great deal of data into account: disciples like Peter and Levi, who physically follow Jesus, are in fact those who leave everything behind (5:11, 27); the rich ruler is told to sell all his goods and then "follow" Jesus (18:23); when the Twelve and the Seventy are told not to carry any provisions or money, they are being commissioned for the itinerant work of proclaiming Jesus' message from village to village (9:1–6; 10:1–11). Conversely, no hint is given that Zacchaeus is supposed to leave his home to follow Jesus (19:1–10), which would explain Jesus' approval of his apparently less-than-exhaustive divestiture; this also accounts for Jesus' affirmation of those who keep their houses and simply offer hospitality to the itinerant disciples (10:5–9). In short, the bi-vocational solution has a great deal to commend it.

Still, there are important elements of Luke's text that the bi-vocational solution does not take into account. Luke 14:33 says that *all* would-be disciples of Jesus have to renounce all their possessions,[13] not just those in "full-time ministry." Likewise, the women disciples in Luke 8 are said to have "provided for [Jesus and the disciples] out of their resources" (8:3), meaning that they did not divest themselves in order to follow Jesus. Indeed, a closer look at Luke 22:35–36 will reveal that even the Twelve did not liquidate all their possessions upon choosing to follow Jesus, and that they normally did have money at their disposal.[14] Finally, the Book of Acts is clear that Paul is gainfully employed and has sufficient funds at his disposal to care for himself, his companions, and the poor in his community (Acts 18:3; 20:34–35), such that one cannot say that becoming an apostle and an evangelist entailed that one divest oneself of all wealth. So the bi-vocational explanation does not solve our problem entirely, but it probably gets us part way there.

The Personalist Explanation

The final perspective in this survey of Lukan scholarship is the *personalist* explanation. Here, advocates point to the inconsistency in Luke's ethics described above and conclude that this intractable diversity should steer us away from looking to Luke for any sort of rules on the proper use of money. Instead, it is argued that Luke sees money as one of the key ways in which one shows one's commitment to God's kingdom; like a spiritual barometer, one's use of possessions reveals one's love of God. Nevertheless, personalists argue that there is flexibility for each adherent of Christianity to decide for him or herself (i.e., *personally*) how to respond to God through one's wealth.

In its favor, this view does indeed describe the way in which most Christians today instinctively engage with the question of wealth. It is also to be commended for rooting the moral issue of money in the more fundamental topic of the love of God, which is the generating center of Luke's ethics.[15] The major vulnerability of this approach, however, is once again that intractable text of Luke 14:33. Certainly, Luke's stern warning that nobody can be Jesus' disciple without renouncing all possessions does seem

The Problems

to run squarely against the flexibility intrinsic to the personalist scheme. Indeed, the ensuing verses of Luke warn that those who shy away from the hard demands of discipleship (salt that loses its saltiness) will be *cast outside* (14:34–35 author's translation). The image of being "cast outside" denotes eschatological punishment in Luke (see 13:25, 28), which should make us very cautious about brushing past the demands of renunciation presented in 14:33.

SUMMARY

In brief, Luke's Gospel is crammed with incendiary, thrilling, and harrowing statements about riches and poverty, justice and judgment. It provides a window on what Jesus says about the sorts of issues that remain flashpoints for contemporary society, and Christians desperately want Jesus to show us a way forward in the dizzying complexity of the twenty-first-century global economy.

However, upon closer inspection, Luke's Jesus can't seem to keep his rules straight. One minute he is telling disciples to divest themselves, and the next he is telling them to bless those who offer them hospitality. Luke apparently shares his protagonist's confusion, oscillating among endorsing almsgiving, divestiture, and (what looks like) socialism. Moreover, much of what Luke and Jesus supposedly endorse look totally unworkable in contemporary society: How can one divest oneself and not become a burden on others? How can one renounce all one's possessions and continue to care for the poor?

Over the past half-century, Lukan scholars have wrestled with this issue, sometimes in ways that appear ludicrously speculative to the nonacademic, and at other times in ways that are promising but do not deal with all the relevant textual data. So the question for us now is: In light of these challenges, is it really meaningful or helpful to speak about Lukan wealth ethics? I think it is.

What follows will help orient us toward *how* to go about understanding the ethics presented in Luke's Gospel.

CHAPTER 2

Toward an Explanation

LET LUKE BE LUKE

THE HERO OF THE TV POLITICAL DRAMA *The West Wing* is President Josiah Bartlet, an intelligent and idealistic character whose first year of office is hamstrung by infighting and at best Pyrrhic victories, in varying degrees selling down the river his values and dreams in order to survive the world of political machination. A key turning point of the first season, however, is an episode when the president's advisors decide to throw prudence to the wind and encourage President Bartlet to be the idealistic visionary who won the office. Their motto becomes *Let Bartlet be Bartlet*.

Sometimes, sitting in pews and in libraries, one gets the feeling that the ethical message of Luke's Gospel is being hamstrung, muzzled. When Luke says, "*Renounce* all your possessions," the scholar says, "*Be willing* to renounce your possessions." Where Jesus tells the rich man that he has to sell all his possessions, the preacher explains that the rich man had a *personal* problem, but that we're not in his situation. When Jesus tells us that camels can sooner pass through the eyes of needles than can rich people enter the kingdom of God, the commentator suggests that perhaps "camel" really means "rope," or that the "needle's eye" refers to a gate in Jerusalem. However well-intentioned these readings may be, they seem to want to save Luke from himself, and one wonders if we could just *Let Luke be Luke*.

After all, if you read Luke as a Christian, he transmits not just his own opinion, but the teachings of Jesus; if you read Luke as a

Christian, his writing reveals something of God. If that is the case, then interpretations intended to "soften" Luke might actually end up silencing Jesus.

But then again, how does a reader know if she is muzzling Jesus or just taking into account the giant gap between a first-century narrative and twenty-first-century society? How do you know if you are silencing Luke or if you are just reading the New Testament as a piece of literature, complete with hyperbole and metaphor?

In our attempt to "let Luke be Luke" while still not pretending that Luke's Gospel or the Book of Acts are handbooks for justice in the twenty-first-century global economy, this short chapter will provide some basic orientation in reading the Gospels as ethical literature. In this way, we'll lay the foundation for an explanation of Lukan wealth ethics.

THE GENRE OF ANCIENT BIOGRAPHY

The first step in thinking about wealth ethics in the Gospel of Luke is to consider its genre, since genre gives us a framework for how to read different pieces of literature and what questions you can or cannot legitimately ask of a given text. For instance, the Book of Job includes various comments about weather (mentioning, for example, that there are storehouses of snow in the sky [Job 38:22]), and yet students of meteorology probably should not consult Job when prepping for an exam. *Little Red Riding Hood* tells of a hunter who slices open a wolf to free an elderly woman and a child, and then fills the beast's belly with stones and sews it back up, but this is not a reasonable guide to taxidermy. These examples seem silly to us, in part because the implicit generic features and limitations of the aforementioned texts are *obvious* to the reader. Things only get complicated when the reader lacks knowledge of the features of a given genre. (This is often the case when people try to read the Book of Revelation, which is an instance of the apocalyptic genre.)

The relevant questions for this study are the following: What sort of literature is Luke's Gospel (we'll talk about the genre of

Toward an Explanation

Acts in chapter 5), and how does that influence our interactions with Luke's comments about money?

Happily, there is a reasonably strong consensus today that the Gospels are examples of ancient biographies, called *bioi* ("lives") in Greek.[1] In the first century, it was common to write biographies of religious figures and philosophers. Those biographies often weave together accounts of the philosopher's teachings with colorful and illustrative anecdotes from that philosopher's life. For this reason, it's often great fun to read biographies of ancient philosophers. For example, in Iamblichus's *Life of Pythagoras* and Diogenes Laertius's biography of the same philosopher, one hears not only about Pythagoras's views of justice and the afterlife, but also about how those teachings led the Pythagoreans to live communally and to refuse steadfastly to touch beans.[2]

The ramifications of this generic identification become quite significant when one begins to think about whether and how ancient biographers thought about *ethics*. Ancient biographers made it clear that they narrated the lives of great people, not just for historical reasons, but also for moral reasons (Plutarch, *Aem.* 1.1–4). In particular, they believed that the examples of their protagonists should be *imitated*.[3] Perhaps the most famous biographer of the first century CE was Plutarch of Caesarea. He explained that by describing both the *teachings* of great men and their *deeds*, he wanted to encourage his readers to imitate their virtue (Plutarch, *Per.* 1.1—2.4; *Cleom.* 131; *Demetr.* 1.6). So ancient biographies were aimed to teach ethics by means of relating what the author's heroes both *said* and *did*.

There are four reasons why this little generic excursus on ancient biographers and their writings is important for our understanding of Lukan wealth ethics. First, these comments on ancient biographies show that it is *legitimate* to read the Gospels (*being ancient biographies*) as *teaching normative ethics*.[4] Second, this data from ancient biographers clarifies that our study of ethics should focus both on the *propositional teachings*[5] of Luke, and also on the *deeds* of his characters, since one would expect the latter to illustrate the former. Third, the *deeds* of Jesus and the apostles are important because the biographer, Luke, expects that readers should *imitate* the laudable example of his heroes.

These comments on imitation do raise an interesting question for us: How precisely should we go about imitating the examples

17

of Jesus and the disciples? Here, Plutarch is helpful again. He clarifies that one should not be overly literal in imitating the characters described in his biographies, but that one should always bear in mind the great difference between the reader's situation and the circumstances of the biography's protagonist.

> When we see little children trying playfully to bind their fathers' shoes on their feet or fit their crowns upon their heads, we only laugh, but the officials in the cities, *when they foolishly urge the people to imitate the deeds, ideals, and actions of their ancestors, however unsuitable they may be to the present times and conditions*, stir up the common folk and, though what they do is laughable, what is done to them is no laughing matter. (Plutarch, *Mor.* 814A)

In other words, even though Plutarch does want his readers to imitate the examples of the heroes whose lives he chronicles, being slavish in the imitation of those people's examples, without recognizing how "unsuitable they may be to the present times and conditions," can do some serious damage.

This teaches us a fourth lesson about how, as biographies, the Gospels teach ethics. While readers are expected to imitate the deeds of the Gospel protagonists, they should do so in a way that takes into account the differences between ancient and modern "times and conditions."

DRAWING PROPOSITIONAL ETHICS FROM NARRATIVE TEXTS

We have seen that, as ancient biography, (1) Luke's Gospel does intend to teach normative ethics; (2) those ethics are to be perceived in both the teachings and actions of the protagonists; (3) readers are supposed to imitate the examples of the Gospel's heroes; and (4) readers are expected to contextualize the imitation of the protagonists in a manner appropriate to their distinct historical and social location. Nonetheless, these observations seem

Toward an Explanation

largely contrary to one of the basic maxims of interpretation one learns in seminary hermeneutics: "Do not draw propositional theology from narrative texts!"

What does this maxim mean and why do seminary professors emphasize it? The rule essentially communicates that just because something happens once in the Bible does not mean that the biblical author is making an implicit promise that this is how things will always work. Just because God parted the Red Sea for Moses does not mean that if you wade in up to your knees, those waters will also recede for you. Just because God delivered Peter from prison does not mean that you won't meet the fate of James the Less (Acts 12). The prohibition of drawing propositional theology from narrative texts is basically a warning not to universalize discrete events as if they were hard and fast rules about how God will consistently and specifically act. In that sense, it is a good reminder to overzealous interpreters.

On the other hand, the four Gospels and Acts are largely narratives (as is 40 percent of the Old Testament[6]), and it is an overreaction to assume that those do not aim to convey to their readers truths about the nature of God, creation, and salvation; how to think about their current situation; and how to live in that light. To do this, narrative authors (including biographers) use a variety of tools, two of which especially warrant our attention: *discourses* and *exemplars*.

In focusing on these tools, we will draw some lessons from the interpretive method of *narrative criticism*. Narrative criticism is an interpretive method that helps us examine how the Gospels work as narratives, in order to teach their readers theology and (as is pertinent for the present book) ethics.

DISCOURSES AND EXEMPLARS

Even though the Gospels and Acts are, broadly speaking, narratives, they are chock-full of *discourses* (i.e., speeches): the teachings of Jesus in the former case and the sermons of Peter, Stephen, and Paul in the latter case. To a significant degree, these discourses are propositional teachings—stating things directly as a general principle or rule—and thus allowing the reader to identify with the narrative audience of the discourse and to apply the principle directly. Accordingly, if you read the Sermon on the Plain and think of yourself as being in some sense part of the audience of those who would be Jesus' disciples (Luke 6:17–20), then you recognize that the Sermon on the Plain speaks to you. Similarly, when Jesus tells the disciples at the Last Supper, "The kings of the Gentiles lord it over them; and those in authority over them are called benefactors. But not so with you; rather the greatest among you must become like the youngest, and the leader like one who serves" (Luke 22:25–26), the reader who is one of Jesus' followers understands that this is a teaching that applies to him or her personally. Most Christian readers of the Gospels do this rather instinctively.

The other tool the New Testament narratives use to communicate theological and moral truths is the narrative *exemplar*, or to use different terminology, the *paradigmatic figure*.[7] Exemplars are like test cases for the ideas being propositionally discussed in the narratives; the relationship between exemplars and discourses is akin to the relationship between showing and telling. Jesus *tells* the disciples that it is no good to gain the whole world but lose their souls, that becoming his followers means dying daily (9:23–24). And Jesus *shows* them what this means, both in smaller ways (such as rejecting acclaim and enduring reproach [4:28–29]) and in the ultimate way (enduring physical death). Thus, exemplars both interpret how a propositional teaching can be realized in a particular situation, and they inspire readers to apply that propositional teaching in their own distinct situations, albeit in distinct ways.

The New Testament authors are sometimes explicit in their intention that the figures of the stories be seen as paradigmatic. So, in the example of the Last Supper mentioned above, Luke's Jesus follows up his propositional teaching on being a downwardly mobile, servant leader with a direct assertion, "I am among you as one who serves" (22:27). His example is to be imitated; he is the paradigm for his own teachings. So also John's version of the same supper describes Jesus washing his disciples' feet and then saying, "So if I, your Lord and Teacher, have washed your feet, you also ought to wash one another's feet. *For I have set you an example, that you also should do as I have done to you*" (John 13:14–15, emphasis mine).

Jesus is far from the only exemplar in the New Testament narratives; sometimes the apostles have the same function. Paul, in his farewell speech to the Ephesian elders, reminds them of how he had "worked with my own hands to support myself and my companions" (Acts 20:34). Paul then specifies that he has reminded them of this fact because they (as well as readers who would in some measure identify themselves with the Ephesian elders who were the addressees of the message) are to follow his example: "In all this *I have given you an example* that by such work we must support the weak" (Acts 20:35, emphasis mine).

Not all exemplary figures are positive. Some characters are negative exemplars, showing the reader what *not* to do, providing a contrast with the behavior modeled by the protagonists. A great example of this contrast occurs early in Acts. Barnabas acts as a *positive exemplar* of the statement in Acts, "There was not a needy person among them, for as many as owned lands or houses sold them and brought the proceeds of what was sold" (4:34); Barnabas himself "sold a field that belonged to him, then brought the money, and laid it at the apostles' feet" (4:37). By contrast, Ananias and Sapphira are *negative* exemplars, embezzling funds from the sale of their land and trying to dupe the apostles (5:1–11). So paradigmatic figures both show the reader what sort of behavior to avoid and what sort of behavior to imitate, how one should and should *not* apply the abstract teachings of the discourses.

In brief, to interpret the ethics of a narrative text, one has to pay attention to both the discourses and the exemplary figures. The paradigmatic figures give examples—illustrations, as it were—of how the narrator himself thinks that the teachings should be understood and applied, or (in the case of negative exemplars) what it looks like to fail to respond properly to the teachings in the discourses. Therefore, it is possible to draw propositional ethics from narrative texts, if indeed you identify with the dramatic audiences of that text. In fact, narrative texts are especially helpful for those who identify with the audiences of the discourses because the narratives also give examples of how one might apply those ethics.

These interpretive insights dovetail neatly with our previous observations about how the genre of ancient biography aims to stimulate its readers ethically. Just as ancient biographies offered anecdotes to illustrate the practical out-workings of their subjects' teachings, so the characters in the Gospel exemplify proper responses to Jesus' sermons. Likewise, the subject of the biography is displayed as a model to be imitated, just as the protagonists of the narratives are positive paradigms, whose examples the readers are expected to follow. Finally, just as narrative critics would hasten to point out that the commands to bear one's cross daily or wash one another's feet can and should generate any number of distinct responses, depending on the reader's context,[8] so also ancient biographers expected their readers to imitate the virtues of the biographies' protagonists in ways appropriate to the reader's historically unique circumstances.

PRESERVING PERSPECTIVE

There is one more point to be born in mind before we turn to give a proper account of Luke's wealth ethics: we need to remember that Luke cares about *more* than just money.

When scholars write academic monographs on a given section of a biblical book, they spend thousands of hours poring over a single topic, or even a single chapter or passage. In so doing, we sometimes forget that the biblical author did not spend anywhere near as much time writing a given verse as we do studying it. To some degree, the extensive study is necessary, since it helps us to learn about the sorts of suppositions and information that shaped the author as he wrote; sometimes we have to work very hard to discover what the author took for granted. But the downside of this detailed approach is that we sometimes imagine that the author intended to communicate much more in a given text than he did. We find deep meaning in every stray definite article, and we perceive symbolism in mundane details, sometimes overlooking the possibility that (as Freud is supposed to have quipped), "Sometimes a cigar is just a cigar."

This is not to deny that Luke was tremendously concerned about money; the fact that he wrote about it with such frequency and in such colorful detail makes it clear that he was passionate

Toward an Explanation

about the topic. The point is rather to remember that Luke's first concern is to write a biography of Jesus' life and teachings (cf. Luke 1:1–4) and that he was concerned about multiple moral topics (including especially suffering and family) alongside any number of theological and historical matters. He addressed all these issues and also attempted to develop a literarily sophisticated narrative. We should bear this in mind when we query Luke about his wealth ethics: money, for Luke, is one important piece of a much larger puzzle. Thus, we may well have questions on money to which Luke does not provide answers.

Finally, we need to remember that Luke sees himself, not just as writing theology or narrative, but as writing a historically true text:

> Since many have undertaken to set down an orderly account of the events that have been fulfilled among us, just as they were handed on to us by those who from the beginning were eyewitnesses and servants of the word, I too decided, after investigating everything carefully from the very first, to write an orderly account. (Luke 1:1–3)

Critical scholars do ask questions about whether all the events in the Gospels are historical (those who are skeptical about miracles tend to doubt that Jesus walked on water or rose from the dead) and whether Jesus said all the things ascribed to him (since Luke includes teachings that one doesn't find attested elsewhere). But, unless we see Luke as deluded or malicious, we should take seriously the fact that the introduction to his Gospel does indicate that Luke made a serious effort to transmit information that he thought derived from Jesus himself. What that means is that we should not think that Luke felt free to make up things that suited his agenda or that might fill in what he perceived to be gaps in, for example, Jesus' wealth ethics.

Sometimes scholars make a big deal about what a text doesn't say, about the "dog that didn't bark." Indeed, it is important to note if Luke drops something from a source that he is clearly copying; that shows he may be trying to sharpen a point.[9] But if his Gospel or Acts don't address a given subject or if they cease to discuss a matter at some point, it may not be because Luke didn't care about the matter; it may simply be that he had no relevant historical material with which to work. In short, we will need to be careful not to make arguments from silence, and also to remember that, in writing his books, Luke had more agendas than simply money.

This chapter has established a conceptual ring in which to wrestle with Luke's wealth ethics, "letting Luke be Luke" in all his stubborn radicality, rather than trying to subdue him with modern sensibility. In order to hear Luke on his own terms, we have to understand what sort of literature we are reading. We have seen that, as an ancient biography of Jesus, we can expect that Luke's Gospel was trying to teach ethics to its readers. It attempted to rouse them to action, to respond to Jesus' teachings, and to imitate his example. We have also seen, thanks in part to narrative criticism, that the narratives include paradigmatic figures that help illustrate some of the right and wrong ways to act in the light of Jesus' teachings. The conventions of both narrative criticism and ancient biography have warned us that the moral teaching of the text aims to generate contextually distinctive responses, rather than slavish copying. Finally, we have been warned against *overreading* Luke and Acts, looking for major meaning in tiny details or expecting levels of comprehensiveness that are not realistic, given Luke's many agendas in writing the book. At this point, we are ready to roll up our sleeves and grapple with Luke's teachings on money.

CHAPTER 3

Total Commitment to God

> I appeal to you therefore, brothers and sisters, by the mercies of God, to present your bodies as a living sacrifice, holy and acceptable to God, which is your spiritual worship. Do not be conformed to this world, but be transformed by the renewing of your minds, so that you may discern what is the will of God—what is good and acceptable and perfect. (Rom 12:1–2)

PAUL TELLS THE ROMAN CHRISTIANS to be mentally transformed so that they can discern God's will…but what if God's will does not seem reasonable to us? What if God's priorities differ from ours? Paul's moral exhortations in Romans (chapters 12—15) begin from the premise that our societal values, the morality into which we are socialized, the morality that seems *reasonable* to us, is likely to be *very different* from God's values. As such, Paul tells the Romans that they have to be "transformed by the renewing of their minds," and he implies that without that transformation, they won't be able to know the will of God, what is good, acceptable, and *perfect*. Indeed, this mental transformation is part and parcel of Paul's plea that the Romans come to see themselves as "living sacrifices."

Living sacrifices; perfection. Paul's vision seems ambitious… but then again, he is trying to speak about the very will of God. The question for us is whether Luke is as idealistic as Paul.

RENOUNCING EVERYTHING

In our last chapter, we noted that Luke has theological and moral agendas beyond wealth ethics. Accordingly, as we explore Lukan wealth ethics, we need first to identify the broad generating center of Luke's ethics. Thereafter, we will be in a better position to analyze the center of Luke's wealth ethics specifically.

THE CENTER OF LUKE'S ETHICS

> You shall love the Lord your God with all your heart, and with all your soul, and with all your strength, and with all your mind; and your neighbor as yourself. (Luke 10:27)

Most New Testament scholars agree that the commandments to love God and love one's neighbor comprise the center of Jesus' moral teaching. After all, each of the Synoptic Gospels includes Jesus' summation of the Old Testament Law in terms of the commands to love God and love one's neighbor. Matthew, for example, introduces this theme after a Pharisee asks Jesus, "Which commandment in the law is the greatest?" After Jesus answers with the compound citation of Deuteronomy 6:5 and Leviticus 19:18, he concludes, "On these two commandments hang all the law and the prophets" (Matt 22:36, 40).

Let's take a closer look at the text cited above (which is called the "double love command"). Jesus begins by saying that the greatest commandment (Deut 6:5, part of the *Shema*, a prayer that faithful Jews recited every morning and every evening) is to love God with *all of one's being*: heart, soul, strength, and mind. Interestingly, some Jews understood the word translated as "strength" to denote, not one's physical power, but one's wealth.[1] That actually seems a sensible decision, insofar as it is easier for me to imagine loving God with my money than with the ability to do dozens of push-ups. But in any scenario, it is clear that Jesus is demanding that God be loved with all that we are and have.

The second element of the commandment is derived from Leviticus 19:18: "You shall love your neighbor as yourself." In Matthew 22:39 and Mark 12:31, this imperative is depicted as a second and subsidiary commandment; the *first* and *primary* commandment is to love God, and the commandment of secondary importance is to love the neighbor. Luke, however, actually rolls the second commandment into the first, depicting the two as *one* commandment. Luke writes a single imperative verb—"You shall love"—that governs *two* direct objects: "the Lord" and "your neighbor." That's why scholars sometimes call this the "double love *command*" (singular), rather than the "love *commands*" (plural). The fusion of both commandments into a single imperative is significant, because it shows that Luke does not consider it credible to claim you love God but fail to love your neighbor; the two go hand-in-hand, for you cannot love God while neglecting your neighbor *whom God also loves as much as you*.[2] Love of God must issue in love of neighbor.

Notice, moreover, the way in which Luke characterizes how followers of Jesus are to love their neighbors: "You shall love your neighbor *as yourself*." God's people are supposed to love their neighbors like they love themselves. This is, on the one hand, almost ridiculous. How can I love my neighbors like I love myself? Even toward my children, whom I love desperately and for whom I would die, I do not consistently behave in a way that is loving; rather, my selfishness often inclines me to put my desire (say, for peace and quiet) in front of their desires (say, to run around the house happily banging on drums). So how reasonable is it to think that I should love my neighbors as myself when I do not even consistently do that with my own kids?

On the other hand, however impractical this imperative may seem, it is also *deeply* logical. Insofar as one assumes that God loves my neighbor as much as he loves me, it stands to reason that God would want my neighbor to be treated as well as I am treated. This is of course the corollary of the Golden Rule: "Do to others as you would have them do to you" (Luke 6:31).

In Luke's version of the scene in which Jesus pronounces the double love command, Jesus is talking to a lawyer (that is, a scribe who is an expert in the Jewish Torah). The chap is ostensibly a savvy interpreter of the Law, and so, when he reacts to Jesus' double love command, the scribe probably has two strategies in mind, two ways to dampen Jesus' apparently unrealistic commandment. First, the lawyer probably knows that, in the context of Leviticus 19, the command to "Love your neighbor as yourself" does not

RENOUNCING EVERYTHING

mean that you have to act with generosity toward your neighbor, but rather that you just cannot do nasty things to your neighbor. After all, notice how Leviticus 19:18 begins: "You shall not take vengeance or bear a grudge against any of your people, but you shall love your neighbor as yourself." Moreover, the preceding verses of Leviticus 19 focus on prohibiting theft, perversion of justice, and hatred (19:11–17). So perhaps the scribe thinks that if he avoids abusing his neighbors, it counts as "loving" them.

Second, the scribe anticipates that he can take the edge off of Jesus' command by circumscribing the definition of the neighbor he is to love: "But wanting to justify himself, he asked Jesus, 'And who is my neighbor?'" (Luke 10:29). This was not, from the lawyer's perspective, an unreasonable question. Most of the scribe's colleagues would have said that only fellow Jews qualified as one's "neighbor"; Samaritans and Gentiles were generally considered nonneighbors. So the scribe hopes that Jesus will limit the scope of the people he has to love.

Jesus answers the scribe's question with the parable of the Good Samaritan (Luke 10:30–35), a story that fleshes out what Jesus considers love of neighbor to entail. Jesus tells of a man (ostensibly Jewish) who gets robbed and beaten within an inch of his life, and then is left for dead. Two Jewish religious leaders spot the wounded man but refuse to help him. (They probably pass by because they can't tell whether or not the man is dead without getting close to him; but if they do stop to check out the man on the side of the road, and he *is* already a corpse, they will have become ritually impure).[3] Thereafter, a Samaritan—who was *not* considered a Jew's neighbor—comes to the rescue and invests his own resources (wine, oil, and money) to save the wounded man's life.

Jesus' key point—and his answer to the scribe's inquiry about who counts as the neighbor that the scribe is supposed to love—comes in verses 36–37. Jesus asks the scribe, "Which of these three men do you think *became a neighbor* to the man who fell among the thieves"; the answer is obviously, "The one who showed him mercy" (my translation).

Most translations fail to highlight that the verb italicized above (in Greek, *gegonenai*) is actually a perfect form of the verb *to become*. Jesus' question is thus: "Which of these three *has become* a neighbor?" This means that Jesus is underscoring that, when the

Samaritan first set out on his journey that morning, he was not a neighbor to the wounded man; but the Samaritan *became* a neighbor to him by showing him kindness. The message to Jesus' listeners is obvious: rather than asking who *is* the neighbor you *have to* love, you should *become* a neighbor to anyone you *can* love. "Go and do likewise" (10:37).

Lovely sentiment, Jesus, but how on earth could that actually be done? It seems that the double love command is indeed as unrealistic as it appeared at first blush: Jesus wants his followers to love, *as themselves*, anyone *to whom they can become a neighbor*, and to show that love by extending their neighbor mercy, especially financial care. This fits with Jesus' teachings in the Sermon on the Plain—"Be merciful, just as your Father is merciful" (Luke 6:36)—but again, does it not seem absurd to say that we should be merciful in the same way that *God* is merciful? That seems just as naïvely idealistic as when Matthew's Sermon on the Mount says, "Be perfect, therefore, as your heavenly Father is perfect" (Matt 5:48).

And yet, however impractical this may seem, we are *not* asking about what sort of morality is *feasible*; we are asking about Luke's ethics, and Luke sees himself as describing Jesus' ethics. More to the point, Jesus sees himself as describing *God's* ethics. He is interested in describing what is *right* from *God's perspective*, and so he must talk about perfection: perfect love, perfect holiness, and perfect mercy. Indeed, when asking about God's ethics, would we really expect to find a morality that is practical and realistic for people who are sinners and thus very much *not like God*?

The generating center of Luke's (and Jesus') social ethics, therefore, is the commandment to love God with all that we are and have, and consequently to love as ourselves the people that God loves just as much as he loves us. According to Luke, that is the goal, impossible and right.

The parable of the Good Samaritan is unique to Luke and that is important for our purposes here, because it shows that Luke sees wealth ethics as part and parcel of the command to love one's neighbor (lest we try to limit the commandment to love our neighbors to purely *emotional* affection). Luke's Jesus says that we are to love, even with our resources, anyone to whom we can become a neighbor.

So we have seen that the center of Luke's ethics generally speaking is *total commitment*—total love—to God and, therefore, love for neighbor as oneself in expression of God's love and mercy. We have also seen Luke's Jesus connect the love of neighbor to the use of one's money, and explicitly say that his listener should "Go and do likewise." So, as we drill down into Luke's moral teachings that focus explicitly on money, it seems logical to ask if there is any other place in Luke where Jesus argues that disciples are to express such *total commitment* in their use of money.

FAMILY, SUFFERING, AND MONEY

Happily (or unfortunately?!), such a text does exist. Jesus elaborates on the core principle of the double love command (total commitment to God with all that one has and is) in Luke 14:25–33, explaining how total commitment to God works itself out in three central areas of life: family, suffering, and money.

> Whoever comes to me and does not hate his father and his mother, and his wife and his children, and his brothers and sisters, and even his own life, cannot be my disciple. Whoever does not carry his cross and follow me cannot be my disciple….Any one of you who does not renounce all of his possessions cannot be my disciple. (Luke 14:25–26, 33, my translation)

These are the big three ethical topics on which Luke focuses in his Gospel. Here he reduces Jesus' teachings to three stark conditions for discipleship.

What all three of these teachings have in common is the fact that they are the outworkings of a total commitment to God above all else. If one loves God with all that one is and has, then one will follow Jesus through much suffering and even to the point of death (14:26). If one loves God to the point of death, then following Jesus will mean that oftentimes it will look as though a person hates their family, insofar as what one does in fidelity to God will not seem to be best for one's spouse and children (14:25).[4] And of course, if one's total commitment to God is so thoroughgoing as to cause one to embrace death and accept even the suffering of one's own family, then it seems obvious that it would also entail one to renounce all possessions, both in order to serve God fully and *also* because loving God issues in loving one's needy neighbors.

These are heavy teachings...but they follow from the generating center of Jesus' ethics: one is to love God with all that one is and has, and one is to love one's neighbor as oneself.

THE SHARP EDGE OF LUKE'S WEALTH ETHICS

So the double love command (Luke 10:27) is the center of Luke's ethics broadly speaking, and the ramifications of that command for family, suffering, and money are played out in their most extreme forms in Luke 14:25–33. Since verse 33 is the one that focuses on the way that total commitment to God impacts one's use of wealth, we would do well to give that verse our close attention. Indeed, the fact that it proved to be one of the perpetual stumbling blocks for other explanations of Luke's wealth ethics (see chapter 1) suggests that if we come to a clear understanding of this verse, it will likely help us to organize our understanding of the rest of Luke's teachings on money.

> Any one of you who does not renounce all of his possessions cannot be my disciple. (Luke 14:25–26, 33, my translation)

To understand this verse clearly, we need to pay attention to two key words, the significance of which is rather less obvious than might appear to be the case at first glance: *all* (*pas*) and *renounce* (*apotassetai*).

WHAT DO YOU MEAN BY *ALL*?

It may seem strange to ask what the word *all* means. It is such a common word that haggling about its meaning may call to mind President Bill Clinton's impeachment proceedings, when he obfuscated before a grand jury over the meaning of the word *is*. Nonetheless, a closer look at the Gospels, and indeed, at our own day-to-day speech, makes it clear that the word *all* does not always mean "each and every one without exception."

In reality, both in contemporary parlance and in the biblical text, the word *all* is a word that is commonly used *hyperbolically* (that is, as an exaggeration). This happens *numerous* times in the Synoptic Gospels.[5] For example, when Luke says "*all* the people would get up early in the morning to listen to [Jesus] in the temple" (21:38), he is implying that *lots* of people would go listen to Jesus in the temple, not that *every inhabitant of the city*, including Pilate and the peasant toddlers and the household servants, would wake up early, abandon their duties, and cram themselves into the temple courts (which would have been spatially impossible).

Similarly, when he writes in Acts, "In the first book, Theophilus, I wrote about *all* that Jesus did and taught from the beginning" (1:1, emphasis mine), Luke does not imply that he gave an *exhaustive* account of each of Jesus' miracles and teachings, but rather that he offered a *thorough* account of Jesus' important discourses and deeds. After all, Luke does not include every saying of Jesus that was present in Matthew's Gospel and Luke also cites an otherwise unattested saying of Jesus in Acts 20:35; Luke knew full well, when writing the preface to Acts, that his Gospel did not include each and every saying and deed of Jesus.[6]

It should not surprise us that the biblical authors use the word *all* in a hyperbolic fashion, exaggerating their point for rhetorical effect. The same phenomenon occurs in Hebrew, in Romantic and Germanic languages, and in English. We *all* do this *all* the time.

Therefore, if Luke 14:33 uses the word *all* hyperbolically, then it does not mean that disciples have to renounce "each and every possession." But on the heels of that clarification, I hasten to add that the hyperbolic use of *all* does not therefore render Luke 14:33 toothless. One uses hyperbole to make a point, to communicate the importance of an idea.[7] Therefore, it would be a gross distortion of Luke's message to conclude that the hyperbolic use of *all* in 14:33 means that Luke really does not expect people to renounce their possessions in a significant way. If Luke did not care greatly about renunciation, *he would not have used hyperbole to discuss it.*

WHAT DO YOU MEAN BY *RENOUNCE*?

The word *renounce* is another key term in Luke 14:33 that requires further exploration. In English as in Greek, the word is rather ambiguous. For example, in English, renouncing one's citizenship is not the same thing as renouncing meat, renouncing one's claim to the throne, or renouncing the devil.

In Greek, the word *apotassomai* is used to describe *temporary* abstinence or *permanent* divestiture of something. In the temporary sense, the historian Josephus describes how the biblical character Esther "*renounced* food and drink and pleasures and for three days she begged God to take pity on her" (Josephus, *Ant.* 11.232). Clearly, the renunciation was only for three days; she did not cease eating and drinking permanently. But in other contexts, the verb is used to describe permanent renunciation, as one might more typically imagine.[8]

So also, the verb *apotassomai* sometimes describes an exclusively *internal* renunciation of something, and other times it describes an internal renunciation that results in a very clear *external* action. In the internal sense, the Greek version of Ecclesiastes 2:20 says, "I once again *renounced in my heart* all the fruit of my labor for which I labored under the sun"; this means that, *in his heart*, the preacher despaired of or ceased to hope in his labors without, for example, ceasing to eat his crops. But in the external sense, we see Philo, in his treatise *De sobrietate* (5), describe how one "renounces" passing out drunk, making a moral decision that leads to a very observable external behavior. In short, ancient authors could use *apotassomai* to describe various forms of renunciation, temporary or permanent, internal or external.

The point of this survey of the various uses of the word *renounce* is *not* to say that Jesus' teaching is meaningless. Rather, the point is that we cannot clearly define what Luke means by "renouncing all your possessions" without more information. So,

RENOUNCING EVERYTHING

how do we go about determining what sort of behaviors Luke would have considered "renouncing possessions" and what extent of renunciation gives the word *all* the weight the hyperbole demands?

The answer will be obvious to any Scripture student, who will know that "context is king." One has to examine the broader context of Luke's writings to see what Luke's Jesus means when he tells us to renounce all possessions. As we saw in last chapter's discussion of how ancient biographies teach ethics, one must pay attention both to what a moral teacher *says*, and to how he and his disciples *behave*, that is, how they flesh out the meaning of their teachings. In the next chapter, we will see how the actions of Jesus and his disciples clarify what Jesus meant when he told his disciples that they must "renounce all" their possessions.

CHAPTER 4

Models of Discipleship in Luke

IF YOU HAVE TO SUM UP THE JESUS' teachings on ethics in Luke's Gospel, they are essentially about total commitment to God (love the Lord your God with all your heart, soul, strength, and mind), which results in loving your neighbor as yourself (since God loves your neighbor and you should be merciful as God is merciful). The consequences of this overarching ethic for money are obvious: total commitment to God and love for your neighbor as yourself means that you should dedicate all your resources to the love of God and neighbor. Simple, right?

Well, the logic is clear. But when Luke envisions people dedicating all their possessions to the kingdom, what exactly does he have in mind? As discussed in chapter 2, we need to examine not only the ideas that Luke *teaches*, but also the behaviors he *describes*. So how does Luke describe the wealth ethics of his protagonists? When he fleshes out what it looks like to renounce all possessions (14:33), what actions does he narrate?

This is where things get tricky: as we saw in chapter 1, Luke does not describe just one form of wealth ethics; he is pretty positive about a variety of different behaviors. It seems like Luke actually thinks that there is more than one way, indeed, that there are many ways, to "renounce all your possessions."

One strategy by which to begin sorting out the different ways Luke approvingly understands renunciation of possessions is by recognizing the difference between itinerant and nonitinerant disciples. As the *bi-vocational* explanation of Luke's wealth ethics points out, Luke does broadly distinguish between these two modes of being a disciple of Jesus: some people embrace his teaching without following him geographically; others follow Jesus' teachings while literally following him around.

In this chapter, we will look at these two groups of disciples, and examine how they exemplify or act as paradigms of total commitment of their wealth to the love of God and neighbor. We will see that even within a given group, different people renounce all in different ways. This will lead us, in turn, to conclude that there is something to be said for the *personalist* explanation of Lukan wealth ethics: not everyone will fit into one (or two) lifestyle boxes, even though that certainly does not mean that anything goes.

THE ITINERANTS

Jesus: Living without a Home

Since Luke's Gospel is an ancient biography, it's probably wise to begin our examination of renunciation of possessions with a look at the biography's central character: Jesus.

Luke makes it clear that Jesus took his own teachings on renouncing possessions seriously, as we can see in Jesus' "recruiting pitch" to one would-be disciple.

> As they were going along the road, someone said to him, "I will follow you wherever you go." And Jesus said to him, "Foxes have holes, and birds of the air have nests; but the Son of Man has nowhere to lay his head." (Luke 9:57–58)

In other words, when a well-meaning person expresses his desire to join the crew of itinerant disciples, Jesus warns him that being on the road and preaching the gospel means that he himself had given up having a house, sometimes having to sleep on the ground and in the elements. Even though animals have their burrows, the

Models of Discipleship in Luke

Son of Man renounced having a home in favor of proclaiming the kingdom.

Some writers go so far as to speak of Jesus' "homelessness," but it may be something of an anachronism to call Jesus homeless, insofar as twenty-first-century society tends to think of homelessness as being the result of (and being characterized by) total indigence. Still, it is not clear that impoverished and homeless is the best way to imagine Jesus during his ministry.

There were indeed itinerant philosophers and religious leaders in the first century who were homeless and intentionally poor; they were called the "Cynics"[1] and the Essenes. The Cynics were philosophers who were all about shedding the conventions of society (both moral and material) and living a form of radical freedom and self-sufficiency, just like animals do. They ate simple food, slept on the ground, owned only a single cloak, and basically lived as mendicant vagabond philosophers, begging for alms in exchange for their teachings.[2] Similarly, among the Jewish people there existed a group known as the Essenes. Some of the Essenes were known for itinerant preaching (at least at times), wearing only a single garment until it positively fell apart, and (in the case of the Qumran community) sharing their possessions communally.[3]

In light of the lifestyles of these two groups, it would not have seemed totally weird if Jesus were an impoverished itinerant beggar. But it would probably be an exaggeration of the evidence to envision Jesus as emaciated and bedecked in rags.[4] As we will see below, Jesus had his needs cared for by a group of women disciples who had some money (Luke 8:1–3), and he is frequently depicted as receiving hospitality (Luke 4:38–39; 5:29; 10:38–40; 11:37–38; 14:1–24; 19:5–6; 22:7–13). That certainly does not mean he stayed at nice hotels or that he always had a full stomach, but it does keep us from imagining him as an indigent ascetic.

Thinking in terms of narrative exemplars (i.e., thinking about how Luke describes characters living out the morality he expounds), Jesus certainly does practice what he preaches about renouncing all possessions. He leaves behind his home and security in order to proclaim the arrival of the kingdom of God. But it probably would be overstating the case to say that he was totally impoverished.

RENOUNCING EVERYTHING

The Twelve Disciples: Leaving Possessions Behind (Mostly)

We get a more detailed glimpse at the financial entailments of "following Jesus" when we examine the actions of the Twelve disciples. A close study of these figures shows that they took Jesus' commandments about renouncing possessions very seriously, even though they did not all have the same lifestyle and even though they did not thoroughly divest themselves of all possessions.

Peter, James, and John

The first disciples recruited in Luke's Gospel are the fishermen, Peter, James, and John. He calls them while they are working, and they witnessed his power manifested in the miraculous catch of fish (5:1–10). Luke then writes, "When they had brought their boats to shore, they left *everything* and followed him" (5:11, emphasis mine).

This text gives us a fascinating insight into Luke's ethics, by means of *redaction criticism*. Redaction criticism is a method of biblical interpretation that looks at how authors use and change their sources. When an author seems to be more or less copying a source, and then suddenly he adds or drops something, it might tell you something about what he wants to communicate. In the case of the present passage, Luke was using Mark 1:16–20 and Matthew 4:18–22 as his sources.[5] But whereas Mark says, "They *left their father Zebedee* in the boat with the hired men, and followed him" (1:20) and Matthew says, "They *left the boat and their father*, and followed him" (4:22), Luke says, "They left *everything* and followed him" (5:11) (emphasis mine).

It is not a coincidence that Luke has replaced the words "their father" and "the boat" with "everything," because the Greek word translated "everything" (*panta*) is the same word that appears in Luke 14:33, when the disciples are told to renounce "all" their possessions.[6] Luke emphasizes that when the disciples decided to follow Jesus, they were not just leaving behind Zebedee and the boat, but *everything*: homes, family, jobs, and so on. In this way, Luke makes it clear that Peter, James, and John were doing precisely what Jesus would tell future disciples to do: renounce *everything* to follow him.

And yet, in spite of this real renunciation, the disciples did not fully *divest* themselves to follow Jesus. They *leave everything behind*. Renunciation takes a variety of forms, and should not be strictly identified with divestiture (which is only one form of renunciation), as we will see below in the case of the rich ruler (Luke 18:18–30). They do not sell their houses, hock their furniture and tools, and put their children on the street; rather, they just walk away. This point will become clearer in the ensuing subsections.

Levi

Later, Jesus comes across a tax collector named Levi. As a tax collector, Levi would have been better off than Peter, James, and John. Since they were fishermen, those disciples would not have been utterly indigent, but they also probably were not taking annual summer holidays to Caesarea Maritima! Being a tax collector, however, meant that Levi had the ability to make a good wage, all while sitting in a tollbooth imposing taxes on merchants that passed by,[7] and sometimes fudging the figure supposedly owed in order to line his own pockets.

Jesus calls Levi (5:27), who rather surprisingly leaps at the opportunity to be Jesus' disciple. Luke describes his reaction much in the same way he did that of Peter, James, and John: "He got up, left everything (*panta*), and followed him" (5:28). Once again, redaction criticism is illuminating. Whereas Luke's source (Mark 2:14) just says, "And he got up and followed him," Luke once again inserts the phrase "left everything." Luke is emphasizing a point: following Jesus means leaving *everything* behind. When Levi leaves behind a secure job to follow Jesus, he becomes a graphic exemplar of what Luke 14:33 will say propositionally: disciples renounce everything for Jesus.

Here's where things get interesting. Immediately after saying that Levi left everything to follow Jesus, Luke tells us that Levi went to his house to throw a big party! "Then Levi gave a great banquet for him in his house" (5:29). This reinforces the point made in the last section: when Luke says that the disciples left everything to follow Jesus, he is *not* saying that they divested themselves to follow Jesus. Rather, he is saying that they left everything *behind*. And yet the repeated insertion of the word *all* at these crucial junctures indicates that Luke does see leaving everything behind as a viable expression of the thing mandated propositionally in 14:33: renouncing all possessions.

Instructions for Itinerant Ministry

Luke fleshes out the details of the disciples' renunciation further with the three passages that detail the instructions Jesus gave his disciples for their itinerant ministry (Luke 9:1–6; 10:1–11; 22:35–38).

On two occasions, Jesus sends out his disciples in pairs (first, commissioning the Twelve, and later, sending off a larger group of seventy) to preach in various villages prior to his arrival, preparing the audiences for "the main event," as it were. The disciples have been following Jesus for some time by this point in the narrative, but preaching only in pairs is a new development. On these two occasions, Jesus clarifies that the disciples should not carry any supplies with them: no shoes, no money, no bag, no change of clothes (9:3; 10:4); they are rather to be like "lambs [in] the midst of wolves" (10:3), trusting in God to provide for their every need (cf. 12:22–28).

The way the disciples are supposed to survive on these trips, in contrast to the way they managed when they were with Jesus, is by depending on their audiences to provide them with food and a place to stay (9:4; 10:5–9). Like the Son of Man, they will be without a place to lay their heads,[8] depending on the hospitality of the villagers to whom they proclaim the arrival of the kingdom.

Some scholars have drawn a straight line between Luke 14:33 and these instructions for itinerant ministry, asserting that to renounce all possessions indeed means to limit oneself to one garment, no money, no shoes, and to preach in complete dependency on God. This reading, however, is only partially right.

It is fair to say that these instructions articulate one expression of how to renounce all possessions as a disciple of Jesus. Nonetheless, Luke 14:33 cannot be limited only to the *itinerant* disciples, but applies to all disciples—after all, it does say *"any one of you who would be my disciple..."*—and these texts clearly indicate that the Twelve and Seventy are the only ones to receive these specific itinerancy instructions. Moreover, later in the Gospel, Luke will also state explicitly that these itinerancy instructions did *not* describe the way that Jesus and the disciples normally operated.

There is a third text in Luke that evokes the itinerancy instructions. Look at the passage that concludes the last supper.

> [Jesus] said to them, "When I sent you out without a purse, bag, or sandals, did you lack anything?" They said, "No, not a thing." He said to them, "But now, the one who has a purse must take it, and likewise a bag. And the one who has no sword must sell his cloak and buy one....They said, "Lord, look, here are two swords." He replied, "It is enough." (Luke 22:35–38)

Since our concern is with wealth ethics and not violence, we will skip over the fascinating question of why Jesus wants the disciples to have swords,[9] in order to make a crucial observation: the disciples did not normally pack as light as they did on the two occasions when they left Jesus and went out to preach in pairs in Luke 9 and 10. In Luke 22, Jesus speaks of those earlier trips as unique past events, not reflective of the way they all lived when they were together as a group. Moreover, he indicates that the disciples' pockets were not totally empty, that they did not divest themselves of all possessions when they left all behind to follow him. Rather, some of them have purses (22:36, in contrast with 9:3 and 10:4) and a couple of them even have swords (22:38, in contrast with 10:3 and with the commandment in 9:3 not even to bring a staff for protection).

All this is to say that, when the disciples left all to follow Jesus, they did *not divest* themselves of all possessions. The minimal packing list Jesus gave them prior to sending them out in pairs was *not* reflective of how they normally lived.

Mary Magdalene, Joanna, and Susanna: Using Possessions Progressively

Even though the disciples packed light (or rather, not at all!) when they went out to preach in pairs, this was not how they generally conducted their itinerant ministry. Well before the sending of the Twelve and the Seventy, Luke had already explained how Jesus and the Twelve survived.

> Soon afterwards he went on through cities and villages, proclaiming and bringing the good news of the kingdom of God. The twelve were with him, as well as some women who had been cured of evil spirits and infirmities: Mary, called Magdalene, from whom seven demons had gone out, and Joanna, the wife of Herod's steward Chuza, and Susanna, and many others, *who provided for them out of their resources.* (8:1–3, emphasis mine)

Jesus' entourage of disciples was bigger than the Twelve; it included (at least) three women: Mary Magdalene, Joanna, and Susanna, who were also witnesses of the crucifixion and the resurrection (23:49; 24:10). Those ladies were not poor; notwithstanding the patriarchalism of that era, women could still own and control significant wealth (see, e.g., Luke 7:37; Acts 16:14). We do not know how Susanna and Mary made their money,[10] but Luke clarifies that Joanna was the wife of Herod's steward, Chuza, and being steward to the king was a very cushy, white-collar job indeed.

So these women, who had discretionary access to not-insignificant funds, lived as itinerant disciples along with Jesus and the Twelve. But instead of leaving behind everything, they carried a good deal of money with them. They used those funds to purchase the necessary food and supplies for Jesus and the disciples on the occasions when hospitality was not forthcoming. They are clearly positive figures in Luke's Gospel, to be counted among the itinerant disciples, and yet the way they go about "renouncing all" is by progressively and regularly giving to support themselves and their traveling companions. Thus, one can see how Luke's use of exemplary figures allows him to flesh out a diversity of ways in which the teaching of Luke 14:33 can be faithfully appropriated.

The Rich Ruler: Divestiture for Charity

All the paradigmatic figures that have hitherto been introduced are *positive* exemplars, people who show what you *should* do. But before concluding our discussion of itinerant disciples in Luke, we should talk about one *negative* exemplar, who shows what Luke thinks a would-be disciple should *not* do.

Shortly before arriving in Jerusalem and completing his earthly ministry, Jesus meets a rich ruler, who asks him how to "inherit eternal life" (18:18). Jesus tells him that, in addition to keeping the commandments (18:20), the ruler should *"sell all that you own and distribute the money to the poor*, and you will have treasure in heaven; then come, follow me" (18:22, emphasis mine).

Jesus clearly calls the man to itinerant discipleship ("come, follow me"). But he tells him that to do so, beyond just leaving everything behind, he should *sell all* his possessions and give the money to the poor. In the case of this rich man, Jesus calls for the renunciation of all possessions to take the form of *divestiture*, not just abandonment.

In chapter 6, we will return to this text and consider more the reasons *why* Luke calls for renunciation. For the present conversation, however, it suffices to say that it was especially important for the rich man to give up his wealth because

a) his great riches could help many poor people—the neighbors he is supposed to love as himself (10:27)—rather than just being locked up in barns and left behind (cf. 12:16–21);
b) his wealth would be a major temptation to turn back from following Jesus (cf. 4; 9:62; 8:14; 14:28–33).

Indeed, the attractions of his wealth proved too much for the rich man.[11] So he becomes a negative exemplar, showing that choosing to keep one's wealth instead of following Jesus is (obviously) the *wrong* response to Jesus' command to renounce all possessions.

This passage of Luke helps weave together the connections that have emerged between the actions of the disciples and Luke 14:33. On the one hand, redaction criticism makes it certain that Luke 14:33 is in view in the account of the rich ruler. This is another story that Luke has taken from Mark, and he transmits the story pretty carefully, but he makes an important change—one which we might now anticipate. Whereas Mark's Jesus tells the rich man, "Sell *what* you own, and give the money to the poor" (Mark 10:21, emphasis mine), Luke's version says, "Sell *all* (*panta*) that you own." Again, Luke adds the word *all*, the same key word that we saw him add in his account of the callings of Peter, James, John, and Levi, and the same word he used in 14:33. He is ruling out any confusion about wealth ethics: being a disciple requires total commitment to God, the renunciation of *all* possessions.

This passage also clarifies that, even though the rich ruler failed to renounce all by *divesting* himself, the other disciples had succeeded where he had dropped the ball, because they had renounced all by *leaving their homes and families behind*. Responding to the rich ruler's failure, Peter points out that he and the other itinerants "have left everything and followed you" (10:28). Jesus, in turn, affirms that Peter and the rest of the disciples have done the right thing, and will be rewarded for it!

> Truly I tell you, there is no one who has left house or brothers or sisters or mother or father or children or fields, for my sake and the sake of the good news, who will not receive a hundredfold now in this age...and in the age to come eternal life. (Mark 10:29–30)

By leaving behind their homes and families, the disciples had secured for themselves *eternal life*, the very eternal life that the rich ruler had hoped to secure for himself when he approached Jesus (Luke 18:18), but which he forfeited because he refused to sell all his possessions and give the money to the poor (18:22–25).

Jesus and his itinerant disciples are paradigmatic figures; they are narrative exemplars that flesh out what Jesus' abstract command to "renounce all possessions" might entail. They show that, hyperbole notwithstanding, the renunciation of all possessions is serious business, extending even as far as leaving behind one's job and family or divesting oneself entirely.

On the other hand, Luke approvingly describes numerous ways that people renounce all their possessions. This diversity makes it clear that there is not just a single correct response to

Jesus' summons: renunciation of possessions can take the form of divesting oneself all at once (the rich ruler), or using one's wealth selflessly but progressively to provide for others (Mary, Joanna, Susanna), or leaving behind everything (Peter, James, and John), even if without actually liquidating all one's property (Levi). Sometimes an appropriate expression of renouncing all for the sake of the kingdom may entail leaving oneself utterly without any resources (as in the instructions for itinerant ministry), but one need not think that is the only way to be an itinerant (22:35–38).

THE NONITINERANTS

In the previous section, we focused on the itinerant disciples of Jesus, who certainly get most of the spotlight in Luke. (That is only to be expected, insofar as the story follows Jesus through his itinerant travels.) But those folks are not the only disciples in Luke's Gospel. Some people embrace Jesus' message *without* becoming itinerant, and the wealth ethics of these nonitinerant disciples enrich our understanding of the ways in which a disciple might renounce all possessions for Jesus.

Zacchaeus: Justice and Generosity

From a literary point of view, Zacchaeus is a tremendously helpful character because he serves as a literary foil for the rich ruler, an account that occurs just a couple paragraphs earlier (18:18–30), and for Levi (5:27–32). Like the ruler of chapter 18, Zacchaeus is rich (19:2). Like Levi, he is a tax collector, but Zacchaeus is a rung higher on the "corporate ladder": he is a *chief* tax collector (19:2), which means that he would have had a bunch of underlings (like Levi) in his employ.[12] This tells us first that Zacchaeus would have been more affluent than Levi (even though the latter would not have been bad off). Second, Zacchaeus would certainly have been considered highly corrupt. After all, he was a leader of tax collectors, who were generally reputed to exploit their countrymen and to collaborate with Roman imperial domination.

Unlike both Levi and the rich ruler, though, Zacchaeus is never called to be an itinerant. Jesus does not say, "Follow me," to Zacchaeus. Rather, Jesus invites himself to Zacchaeus's house for dinner, and in the context of that dinner pronounces, "Today salvation has come to this house," without Zacchaeus ever indicating any intention to follow Jesus. What this means, from Luke's perspective, is that it is perfectly possible to be a saved disciple of Jesus without becoming itinerant. Consequently, it is very interesting to look at Zacchaeus's wealth ethics and to inquire how Zacchaeus can be seen as "renouncing all possessions" in the manner required by Luke 14:33.

When Jesus went to Zacchaeus's house for dinner, the other citizens of Jericho were galled (19:7); after all, in their eyes, Zacchaeus was a bad person. So Zacchaeus decided to address the elephant in the room: that he got rich by collaborating with Rome (at very least) and perhaps enlarged his profit margins by squeezing his fellow countryman (or taking a cut from his employees, who did the squeezing for him). In response, Zacchaeus volunteers: "Look, half of my possessions, Lord, I will give to the poor; and if I have defrauded anyone of anything, I will pay back four times as much" (19:8).

Some scholars have pitted this text against Luke 14:33 or the example of the rich ruler, arguing that Zacchaeus proves that Jesus does not expect people to renounce "all" possessions. But that is a premature conclusion, even if those scholars are right to perceive the connections between the aforementioned three texts: the passages have important similarities and differences.

Like the rich ruler, Zacchaeus is extremely affluent, which means that, like the rich ruler, it would not be possible for him to embrace the total commitment of discipleship of Jesus without using his wealth to significantly and practically express his love of neighbor by caring for the needs of the poor (cf. 10:27). Unlike the rich ruler, however, the folks in Zacchaeus's city consider it common knowledge that his great wealth owes at least partially to his exploitative activity. So more than just divesting himself charitably, Zacchaeus knows he has an obligation to make amends for his injustices.

For this reason, Zacchaeus declares that he will compensate fourfold anyone he has wronged.[13] He wants to show repentance for his sins and to make things right. This action, however, militates against the thesis that Zacchaeus only renounces half of his possessions; to the contrary, he could only give half of his funds to the poor because he needed to keep some money to compensate those he had extorted.

We should not think that Zacchaeus actually had an itemized record of how much money he had made by exploiting others. Still, it merits clarification that if only 12.5 percent of Zacchaeus's wealth came from malfeasance (this would have probably been a low-ball figure in the eyes of a first-century reader), a fourfold restitution would amount to a full 50 percent of his total value—the other half of the money he was not giving to the poor. Luke's purpose in this story is not to offer a strict accounting of Zacchaeus's redistribution. Rather, Luke uses easy, round numbers to indicate two things:

1. Zacchaeus wanted to give generously and self-sacrificially to help his neighbor, and
2. Zacchaeus was serious about paying for whatever financial crime he might have committed.

If he were to give all to the poor, that would leave open the matter of whether he had made restitution for his malfeasance; but if he had only promised, say, 25 percent of his money to the poor, that would make him look as though he were not actually serious about loving his neighbor. It is important that Zacchaeus shows himself to be equally committed to justice *and* mercy. So Luke uses the 50/50 split between generosity and restitution to make it clear that Zacchaeus was really serious about being Jesus' disciple (*à la* Luke 14:33), even though that meant he was basically going to lose all of his money. In light of this commitment, Jesus announces that Zacchaeus has indeed been saved (19:9).

In Zacchaeus's case, therefore, we have a clear example of a wealthy, nonitinerant disciple who does what the rich ruler failed to do (majorly divesting himself to care for the poor) while also attending to the factors his own past uniquely required: offering justice to those he had wronged. Renunciation of all possessions thus takes a distinct form in Zacchaeus's case, but it's renunciation of all possessions just the same.

RENOUNCING EVERYTHING

The Poor Widow

Complementing the story of the rich tax collector, Luke includes the account of the poor widow in the temple (21:1–4). She is an interesting character for the purposes of this chapter because we have no reason to think that she is an itinerant (the women who are specified to have traveled with Jesus are not poor; 8:1–3), or even a disciple, and yet her wealth ethics is explicitly commended by Jesus. She helps fill in our picture of what sort of use of money Jesus would commend for nonitinerants.

The temple treasury was located in the Court of the Women and it had thirteen horn-shaped receptacles, each dedicated to supporting some distinct aspect of the temple's function. The widow in the story is utterly indigent and the two small coins she drops in (21:2) amount to a total of one sixty-fourth of a denarius (a denarius is more or less a day's wage for a manual laborer); that sum would not have even sufficed to buy her food for a meal upon departing the temple courts. This quantity pales in comparison to the sums being donated by the affluent worshippers around her, but as a percentage of her liquid wealth, it represents everything she has.[14]

Witnessing this scene, Jesus reiterates the point we have seen repeatedly throughout the Gospel: God is looking for total commitment.

> Truly I tell you, this poor widow has put in more than all of them; for all of them have contributed out of their abundance, but she out of her poverty has put in *all* (*panta*) she had to live on. (Luke 21:3–4, emphasis mine)

Once again using the word *all* that has cropped up repeatedly in Luke's wealth ethics, Jesus makes it clear that the sum that one gives is not of primary interest to God. It is not a matter of how much one gives, but of how much one keeps, because one is to love God with *all* one's heart, and soul, and strength (or money, see chapter 3) and mind. The widow exemplifies this total commitment to the love of God.

Models of Discipleship in Luke

Sons of Peace

There is one other group that warrants some comment in order to complete our picture of what sort of nonitinerant discipleship Luke envisions. As we saw in the instructions on itinerancy to the disciples, when Jesus sent out the Twelve and Seventy, he told them to rely on the hospitality of those to whom they preach, accepting their food and their shelter as God's means of provision for their needs (9:4; 10:5–9).

Whether or not the disciples' hosts should be considered "converts" to Jesus' message or his "disciples" is not clear in these texts, but the texts are at very least positive about these hosts.

> Whatever house you enter, first say, "Peace to this house!" And if anyone is there who shares in peace [lit. *if a son of peace might be there*], your peace will rest on that person....Remain in the same house, eating and drinking whatever they provide, for the laborer deserves to be paid. Do not move about from house to house. Whenever you enter a town and its people welcome you, eat what is set before you; cure the sick who are there, and say to them, "The kingdom of God has come near to you." But whenever you enter a town and they do not welcome you, go out into its streets and say, "Even the dust of your town that clings to our feet, we wipe off in protest against you. Yet know this: the kingdom of God has come near." (Luke 10:5–11)

The fact that Jesus describes such hosts as "sons of peace" and tells the disciples to extend their ministry of preaching and healing to the village on the basis of the host's hospitality implies that he approves of the host's behavior. Jesus indicates here that he thinks it good and proper that these villagers, who are certainly nonitinerant, put their houses and incomes to the use of caring for the itinerants. This would argue against a reading of Luke that thinks that total commitment to the kingdom necessarily entails the complete divestiture of all possessions, including homes: Luke frequently depicts Jesus and the disciples as willing recipients of hospitality in the homes of people like Levi, Zacchaeus, and the "sons of peace."

There is, of course, a great deal left unsaid about these sons of peace: we do not know if the group should be considered "disciples" in a strong sense of the word; we do not hear a word about any other aspect of their wealth ethics (almsgiving, tithing, divestiture, and so on). So we need to resist the temptation to fill in what is unsaid with speculation. All this text confirms for us is that Luke's Jesus does not call everyone who hears his message to become an itinerant, and that he approves of nonitinerants having homes and jobs that they use to support the ministers of the kingdom. Caring for such people is an expression of commitment to God, not to mention an expression of love of neighbor. In this way, there is a certain *complementarity* between the itinerants and the nonitinerants, as the former often depend on the latter for hospitality in order to be able to continue their ministry. (This dynamic continues to unfold in Acts; see chapter 5.)

This does not mean, by any stretch, that Luke's Jesus would say that a nonitinerant disciple has no other wealth-ethical obligations beyond offering hospitality. That would go directly against the propositional statement of Luke 14:33, would contrast sharply with the examples of Zacchaeus and the poor widow, and indeed would well out-run the sparse evidence of Luke 9 and 10. This text just shows us that nonitinerants can have homes and jobs without thereby neglecting Jesus' commandment to love God with all they are and have, and to love their neighbors as themselves.

THE HARMONY OF LUKE'S WEALTH ETHICS

Harmony does not entail that every musician plays the same notes; the difference between harmony and dissonance, however, is that in a harmony, the distinct notes correspond to the controlling melody. Luke's discussions of wealth ethics certainly play a wide range of notes, but that diversity produces a complementary harmony rather than an insuperable dissonance.

Models of Discipleship in Luke

The controlling melody of Luke's ethics is the double love command: loving God with all one is and has, and loving one's neighbor as oneself. The logical outworking of this total love of God in financial terms is total commitment of one's resources to God. Luke enjoins this total dedication in propositional and negative terms in 14:33 (renounce all possessions). But the broader context of Luke makes it clear that this renunciation is not about just abandoning possessions, but is also about *using* those possessions rightly.

Just as varying harmonies can elaborate a single melody, so in ancient narratives, numerous exemplary behaviors of characters can elaborate a single moral teaching. In accordance with the *bi-vocational* explanation of Luke's wealth ethics (see chapter 1), we have seen that Luke's Jesus does envision a certain diversity in modes of discipleship: some become itinerant, literally following Jesus, while others follow Jesus figuratively, putting his moral teachings into practice in part by offering hospitality for the itinerants. The disciples are not all "playing the same notes," but they are playing complementary ones; the complementarity of their vocations contributes to the harmony of Luke's wealth ethics.

Still, we can go one step beyond the bi-vocational explanation, because one cannot reduce the lifestyles affirmed by Luke to a pair (the itinerant and the nonitinerant). Some itinerants, for example, leave homes, jobs, and families behind *without* divesting themselves; others *do* divest themselves; and still others use their funds *progressively* to support their itinerancy and their coworkers. The variety of lifestyles has to do with the fact that the disciples have different pasts and different amounts of money. Peter didn't have nearly as much money as the rich ruler did, and so Peter just *left everything behind* to follow Jesus; but the rich ruler needed to *give* his wealth to the poor, putting his affluence to good use. Zacchaeus was rich like the ruler, but because he had been guilty of injustice—unlike the ruler, who kept the commandments (18:21)—Zacchaeus couldn't just give all his money to the poor; he also had to make restitution for his previous extortion. In other words, the disciples' relative wealth and unique paths require their respective renunciations to take different forms. These distinct behaviors manifest the value of the *personalist* explanation of Lukan wealth ethics (see chapter 1). Even beyond the basic

RENOUNCING EVERYTHING

division between itinerant and nonitinerant lifestyles, the specific shape of one's wealth ethic does depend on factors unique to each person.

This affirmation of an element of the personalist explanation does not mean that Luke is self-contradictory: the different wealth-ethical practices affirmed in Luke—abandoning one's home, or divesting oneself, or progressively using one's resources to support the ministry of others, or balancing generosity with restitution—can still be seen as distinct expressions of the same total commitment to God. The distinct behaviors of specific disciples (both itinerant and nonitinerant) are—to extend the musical metaphor a bit further—like unique instruments that nonetheless contribute to their respective harmonies, harmonies that themselves correspond to and enrich the one melody. Itinerancy and nonitinerancy are two different vocational harmonies played by unique and diverse instruments, each according to the disciple's particular financial and biographical situation, but all serving the same melody of loving God with all one's heart, soul, mind, and strength.

CHAPTER 5

Models of Discipleship in Acts

SO FAR, WE HAVE PRIMARILY FOCUSED on Luke's Gospel. Let us now examine the Acts of the Apostles to determine its bearing on the subject of Luke's wealth ethics.

For some interpretations of Luke's wealth ethics, Acts has been like a wrench in the works for two reasons:

1. In the first half of Acts, it looks like the Jerusalem community is practicing some sort of Christian socialism.
2. In the second half of Acts, the subject of money gets far less attention; this makes some scholars conclude that, even though wealth ethics may have been a hobby horse for Jesus, it isn't such a big deal for Luke.

In this chapter, we'll address these questions and ask more broadly whether the wealth ethics of Acts fits with the scheme of total commitment that we saw in the Gospel.

PROLEGOMENA

Before we begin, there are two matters of *prolegomena* (things that need to be said first) that require some comment: the relationship between Luke and Acts, and the genre of Acts.

RENOUNCING EVERYTHING

"Luke-Acts" or "Luke & Acts"?

On the first count, let's talk about the "hyphen war" in Lukan scholarship. Over the course of the twentieth century, scholars increasingly recognized that there is a great deal of narrative and theological continuity between Luke and Acts, and that the Book of Acts seemed to be structured in a way that depends on Luke. In fact, most Lukan scholars have come to think that Luke and Acts were actually two books of one single large volume, part one and part two, if you will. Those emphasizing the integral connection between the books refer to them jointly as the book "Luke-Acts," with the hyphen between the two halves of the title.[1]

Other scholars (myself included) are dubious of the hyphen. While we agree that the same person wrote both books and that Acts intentionally picks up where Luke left off, we think it is probably an overstatement that Luke and Acts are two halves of one work that have to be read conjointly. In other words, we want to drop the hyphen and maintain the distinction between the Books of Luke and Acts.

The reason for favoring the ampersand (that is, the *&* symbol) over the hyphen is that there is no manuscript evidence that Luke and Acts ever circulated together. Additionally, none of the early Christian canon lists[2] ever group Luke and Acts side-by-side. In other words, if Luke wanted us to read the Gospel with Acts, it is not clear that the early Church picked up on that intention.[3]

This may seem like academic hair-splitting, but this distinction is relevant because it helps explain some of the differences between the centrality of wealth ethics in the Gospel and the diminished emphasis money receives in Acts. Whereas dealing with money is a top priority for the Gospel, it is more of a side theme in Acts. If Luke and Acts were intended to be one book, that disparity would be confusing (and perhaps push us to downplay the importance of wealth ethics to the Evangelist). But if these are different books, it would not be odd for them to have different agendas and that wealth would take a couple of steps back in Acts.

The Genre of Acts

Now, if Luke and Acts are two separate books, then we do not need to assume that they have the same genre. This is helpful,

Models of Discipleship in Acts

for while Luke's Gospel is a biography of Jesus (see chapter 2), Acts does not read like one. Instead, Acts deals with a number of different main figures, most prominently Peter and Paul (although Stephen and Philip both get the spotlight for a while); moreover, we don't hear any information about the births or deaths of Peter and Paul, which tend to be rather important elements of ancient biographies. Happily, we do know that it was not strange, in the ancient literary world, to follow up a biography with another book chronicling the acts of the successors of the biography's protagonist. For example, after the historian Diodorus Siculus wrote a biography of Alexander the Great, he also wrote the "Acts" of Alexander's successors.[4]

In mild contrast to the Gospel (which is an ancient biography), it is probably most wise to categorize Acts as a piece of *ancient historiography*. This genre aims not just to describe a series of past events, but to show the diverse causes of history's progress. Accordingly, the Book of Acts chronicles a crucial epoch in the history of Israel after the death of Jesus and shows that God's providence is behind the important transitions that occurred in those decades.[5] Ancient historiography is, however, a flexible genre, and can easily incorporate elements of biography or historical speeches like those we witness in Acts (that's why Diodorus's giant history can still embed a full biography of Alexander).[6]

How does classifying Acts as "historiography" influence our understanding of its ethics? On the one hand, being "history" does constrain Luke's ethical teaching, insofar as he can only include things that he actually thinks happened in history; he does not get to fabricate events just because they would serve his purposes. So, if Luke does not talk about wealth ethics as much in Acts as he did in his Gospel, it may just be because he had less material with which to work.

On the other hand, categorizing Acts as historiography does not *exclude* that Luke might be concerned with moral issues. Ancient historiographies often function to vindicate the moral order—at least as far as the writer understood it—or to offer moral examples, accounts of good people to be imitated and bad people to be repudiated.[7] We can see that Luke, writing from the perspective of Jewish-Christian religion, wants to vindicate the Christian moral order[8] and to offer examples of behavior to be both imitated (e.g., Peter, Paul, and Barnabas) and avoided (e.g., Simon Magus, Ananias and Sapphira).

This shows us that historiography and biography overlap a good deal in the way they teach ethics. Ancient biographies and histories both attempt to stimulate the morality of their audiences by depicting positive figures to be imitated and negative figures to be avoided. Therefore, just as we paid attention to the behavior of Jesus and the disciples in trying to interpret Jesus' teachings on money, so also in Acts we should keep a close eye on the types of wealth-ethical behaviors that are either endorsed or punished.

Now that we have an idea of how Luke and Acts are related and how the historiographic genre of Acts orients our expectations about its moral teachings, we can examine the text.

THE JERUSALEM COMMUNITY

Early in the Book of Acts (2:42–47; 4:30–35), Luke celebrates how the early Jerusalem community flourished, even amidst initial hostilities. He highlights the believers' life of prayer, worship, and most interestingly for the present purposes, the fact that they "had all their possessions in common." Twice, in fact, does Luke emphasize this point, and on the surface, it sounds like Luke is describing some sort of early Christian socialism.

> All who believed were together and had all things in common (*hapanta koina*); they would sell their possessions and goods and distribute the proceeds to all, as any had need. (Acts 2:44–45)

> Now the whole group of those who believed were of one heart and soul, and no one claimed that any possessions were their own, but *everything they owned was held in common (hapanta koina)*....There was not a needy person among them, for as many as owned lands or houses sold them and brought the proceeds of what was sold. They laid it at the apostles' feet, and it was distributed to each as any had need. (Acts 4:32, 34–35, NRSV with adjustments by author)

Models of Discipleship in Acts

Luke leaves little room for doubt that the behavior of the Jerusalem community is, in his mind, exemplary. By selling their possessions and giving the proceeds to the needy, the community is doing exactly what Jesus commanded in Luke 12:33: "Sell your possessions, and give alms." In addition, they ate their meals together daily (Acts 2:46), which is a major economic boon in a preindustrial agrarian society, where the majority of poor people's daily income typically was spent on the next day's food. In fact, the Jerusalem believers were so diligent in their care for one another that nobody among them was in need (4:34). Not only is this just a good thing in its own right, but Luke uses this fact to show that the Jerusalem Christians were experiencing the blessedness that Deuteronomy promised would attend God's people when they obeyed his laws:

> There will, however, be no one in need among you, because the LORD is sure to bless you in the land that the LORD your God is giving you as a possession to occupy, if only you will obey the LORD your God by diligently observing this entire commandment that I command you today. (Deut 15:4–5)

So Luke clearly thinks that the Jerusalem community's wealth ethics are exemplary. But that makes it all the more poignant to ask what it means to have "all things in common."

In the first instance, this text seems to indicate that the early Christians shared their possessions communally ("no one claimed private ownership of any possessions" [Acts 4:32]). So should we imagine this as an early form of Christian socialism? (I have to admit, early in my studies, my inner Ché Guevara hoped this would be the case!)

It is of course anachronistic to think of this behavior in the modern terms of "communism" or "socialism," but there was a first-century Jewish community (the Essenes) that practiced a form of communalism,[9] and so some scholars have suggested that the early Christians themselves implemented a similar community of goods.[10] The problem, however, is that Luke's descriptions of the Jerusalem Christians' behavior does not seem to square with that sort of complete communal sharing. When Luke describes the actions of the Jerusalem Christians, he uses verbs in the imperfect tense (*eichon, epipraskon, diemerizon, eichen, metelambanon* [2:44–46], *hupērchon, epheron, etithoun, diedideto, eichen* [4:34–35]). The imperfect tense indicates habitual or repeated behavior in the past; if Luke wanted to say that the Christians sold off all their goods at once and pooled them communally, he would have used the aorist tense (which is like the "preterite" in modern Romance languages). So the verb tense used in Acts indicates a *continuous* divestiture of wealth, selling of a house or a bit of land as need arose in the community (cf. 2:45; 4:35).

This impression is confirmed, as we will see, by the accounts of Barnabas and the married couple Ananias and Sapphira. These are the only people specifically described as doing what Luke narrates in 2:44–45; 4:33–35. But Luke says that each of them only sold *a piece of property* (4:37; 5:1); while it is perfectly plausible that they did not own any other fields, Luke does not say that they liquidated the rest of their possessions. So Acts does not describe communalism; rather Luke was indicating that the affluent would periodically sell off assets in order to make funds available for the apostles to provide for the periodic or perpetual needs of the poor (4:37; 5:2).

But what about that phrase "all things in common" (2:44; 4:32)? Does that not indicate common property? Probably not, actually! With this turn of phrase, Luke is actually alluding to a common proverb from the Hellenistic world: "Friends have all things in common" (*koina ta philōn*). This proverb (which scholars call the "friendship maxim") was quite widespread, but it probably originated in Pythagorean circles[11] and was more widely disseminated by Platonists.[12] Fascinatingly, on the one hand, both these philosophies *did* advocate a sort of communalism, at least in certain limited contexts.[13] On the other hand, Pythagoreanism and Platonism were developed centuries before Luke wrote, and in the first century, they were definitely in the philosophical minority. Platonism would make a big comeback in the next couple of centuries, but in Luke's day, the leading schools of philosophy were Epicureanism and Stoicism (cf. Acts 17:18).

The friendship maxim was not the exclusive domain of the Pythagoreans and Platonists; it was also widely used by other philosophical schools, including Aristotelianism and Stoicism.[14] Both of these latter schools are quite clear, however, that when they say that "friends have all things in common," they mean that *friends share their possessions freely, without dissolving the notion of private property*. Aristotle and the Stoics agreed that people had the right to own and control their own private property, which in turn enabled them to share their property voluntarily, especially with their friends.

> For individuals while owning their property privately put their own possessions at the service of their friends and make use of their friends' possessions as common property....*It is clear therefore that it is better for possession to be privately owned but to make them common property in use.*[15]

Common use rather than common ownership was the key distinction.

If Pythagoras and Plato used the friendship maxim in a communal way, and Aristotle and the Stoics used it in a noncommunal way, how should we imagine that Luke used it? Setting aside the fact that Stoicism and Aristotelianism were far more popular than Platonism and Pythagoreanism in the first century, Luke himself gives indications that he is thinking in terms more akin to Aristotelianism.

First, the passages of Acts we are considering include an allusion to another Aristotelian maxim. When Luke says that the Jerusalem Christians were "of one heart and soul" (4:32), he alludes to another of Aristotle's sayings about friendship; Aristotle said that friends are "a single soul."[16] Luke seems to have had Aristotle on the brain when writing these texts. Second, the descriptions of the Jerusalem community as meeting in one another's houses and sharing meals together (2:46) fit neatly with Aristotle's idea of common use with private ownership. So it seems more natural to argue that Acts 2 and 4 describe a fantastic Aristotelian form of sharing in the Jerusalem community, as the believers opened their homes and tables freely to one another, and even progressively divested themselves of possessions, in order to care for the needy.

How does this text square with the notion that disciples are to renounce all of their possessions in order to be totally committed to God and to love their neighbors as themselves? In this new phase of their ministry, when the Twelve have ceased to be itinerant and now live in Jerusalem (with very little money; cf. Acts 3:6), they still lead the community around them into an ethic of total commitment. These believers' renunciation of "all possessions" is manifested in the fact that they share all possessions in common. Notice that the key word, *all*, has emerged again in the phrase "*all things* in common." The disciples open their homes and tables to those in need, which calls to mind the instructions on itinerancy of Luke 9 and 10 in the previous chapter. And when the need arises, the believers do not shy away from divesting themselves of property, as the rich ruler of Luke 18 failed to do and as Jesus commanded in Luke 12:33.

In brief, the Jerusalem community functions as another exemplar of Luke's wealth ethics. Those believers practice their discipleship in submission to Luke 14:33, but they realize that total commitment of possessions in diverse ways that depend on their personal situations.

BARNABAS, ANANIAS, AND SAPPHIRA

We have already touched on some other exemplars of wealth ethics in Acts: Barnabas, Ananias, and Sapphira. Barnabas is obviously a *positive exemplar* of wealth ethics; he practices (partial but substantial) divestiture in order to serve the needs of the poor in the community (4:36–37), selling a field so that the apostles can distribute all the proceeds to the needy. On the flip side, Ananias and Sapphira are *negative exemplars*, people who exemplify the wrong sort of wealth ethics. They sold a piece of property, and when they went to give the money to the apostles, they lied about the amount for which it was sold, only giving a portion of the proceeds to the apostles (5:1–2).

On the face of it, Ananias and Sapphira did something remarkably generous; if someone today sold a piece of property and gave a major portion of the proceeds to the needy in the Church, they might get their name on a plaque! Peter, however, indicts them on two counts: for lying and for "embezzling" (*nosphisasthai*).

"Ananias," Peter asked, "why has Satan filled your heart *to lie* to the Holy Spirit and *to keep back* (*nosphisasthai*)

Models of Discipleship in Acts

> part of the proceeds of the land? While it remained unsold, did it not remain your own? And after it was sold, were not the proceeds at your disposal? How is it that you have contrived this deed in your heart? You did not lie to us but to God!" (5:3–4, emphasis mine)

As a result of this deceptive withholding of a portion of the funds, God strikes Ananias down (5:5). Sapphira is then called, and when she confirms her complicity with Ananias, she too is killed (5:8–10).

The payoff of this text for our inquiry is obvious. Ananias and Sapphira leave no doubt that they have not renounced all their possessions nor totally committed themselves and their wealth to the kingdom. If they had, they certainly wouldn't have withheld a portion of the proceeds and lied about it. This makes it clear that total commitment to the kingdom is essential, not just significant generosity. Once again, we see that Luke 14:33 is far more central to Luke's wealth ethics than people typically countenance.

We might want to object to this text; to us modern readers, it seems very harsh indeed. Since the narrative does indirectly cast a rather unflattering light on the generosity of most modern readers (I've never sold a house or a field to feed the hungry!), some have been tempted to say that Ananias and Sapphira are not killed for holding back the money, but for lying about it. It is not clear why that explanation is supposed to be comforting. (Is lying any less of a problem today than greed?) In any scenario, though, that reading ignores the syntax of Peter's accusation. In 5:3, Peter uses two coordinated infinitives—"to lie" and "to embezzle"—to describe what Satan moved Ananias to do. It is for *both deeds together* that Ananias and Sapphira are killed.

The fact that this punishment strikes us as brutal confirms how different our values are from those of Luke's God (we will explore the "theo-logic" of Luke's wealth ethics further in chapter 6). Luke's God blinds his enemies for speaking against the apostles (Acts 13:11; cf. 9:8–9), and he even makes priests mute for questioning fantastic prophecies (Luke 1:20–22). Judas is struck dead because he sold Jesus out for money (Acts 1:16–20; Luke 22:5), and Herod is killed for idolatry (Acts 12:23). Luke feels that no idolatry is as pernicious as the idolatry of money, which is why he warns, "You cannot serve God and wealth" (Luke 16:13). Luke's God sends people to hell for hording possessions and neglecting the poor (Luke 12:16–21; 16:19–31; cf. Matt 25:31–46).[17] Indeed, the verses immediately after Luke 14:33 make it clear that the one who fails to renounce all possessions becomes useless to the kingdom, fit only to be cast "outside" (14:34–35).[18] But if Ananias and Sapphira made anything clear, it is that their allegiance is divided between God and money, that they have not renounced all possessions, and that they are not totally committed to the kingdom. As a result, they are struck down and cast outside.

PAUL

The Apostle Paul is the hero of the second half of Acts, so it should come as no surprise that Luke also depicts him as exemplary in his use of money. In his farewell speech at Miletus, Paul says to the Ephesian elders,

> You know for yourselves that I worked with my own hands to support myself and my companions. In all this I have given you an example that by such work we must support the weak, remembering the words of the Lord Jesus, for he himself said, "It is more blessed to give than to receive." (Acts 20:34–35)

In this text, Paul reminds the Ephesians of how he lived during the two and a half years he ministered in their city. Interestingly, this was a *non*itinerant phase of Paul's ministry. When traveling itinerantly, Paul would accept hospitality from local believers—such as Lydia, Philip, and Mnason (16:15; 21:8–10, 16)—in a way that recalls again the instructions for itinerancy of Luke 9 and 10; we know from his letters that he also received occasional monetary gifts to sustain him during his missionary travels (2 Cor 11:8–9; Phil 4:10–11). But during his nonitinerant period, Paul was engaged in gainful labor as a tentmaker (as was the case during his year and a half in Corinth [Acts 18:2–3; cf. 1 Cor 4:12; 9:4–12; 1 Thess 2:9]), working a regular job and using the afternoon *siesta* each day to preach and discuss the gospel (Acts 19:9).

Note how Paul puts his gainful employment to use: he supports himself and his traveling companions, *and* he helps care for the needy in the community (20:34). Indeed, Paul makes it clear that he intends for his behavior to be exemplary ("In this I have given you an example..."). Furthermore, by quoting Jesus in verse 35, Paul roots his ethics in Jesus' own teachings on generosity.[19] Additionally, the practice Paul describes indicates that he totally committed his possessions to the work of the kingdom, per Luke 10:27 and 14:33. Being a tentmaker was a more lucrative job than being a fieldworker, but it hardly would have generated major income surpluses; the fact that Paul supported a number of other people besides himself bespeaks the thoroughgoing nature of his commitment. In this he serves as an exemplary nonitinerant, working to care for the needy rather than to enhance his own surplus.

OTHER DISCIPLES

What about the wealth ethics of the other disciples described in Acts? Are they exemplary or not? It is probably most balanced to say that there are elements of other disciples' wealth ethics that are endorsed, even if the entirety of their lifestyles do not receive clear comment. For example, Luke clearly affirms the generous almsgiving of Tabitha and Cornelius. As a consequence of Tabitha's generosity to the widows, she is raised from the dead (Acts 9:36–41); for Cornelius's almsgiving, the centurion receives the opportunity to be Peter's first Gentile convert (10:2–6, 31–32). Similarly, Luke applauds the generosity of the Antiochian Church in sending a collection to support the poor in Jerusalem in a time of famine, each person giving "according to their ability" (Acts 11:27–30). Acts likewise reflects the Gospel's emphasis on how nonitinerants should provide hospitality for itinerants (Acts 9:43; 10:32, 48; 16:5; 17:5–6; 18:2–3; 21:8–10, 16).

On the flip side of the same coin, the "villains" of Acts tend to exemplify the greed against which the Gospel repeatedly warns (Luke 8:14; 11:39; 12:15; 16:13). Consider Simon Magus (Acts 8:9–24), the owners of the slave girl with the spirit of divination (Acts 16:16–19), Demetrius the Ephesian silversmith (19:25–27),

RENOUNCING EVERYTHING

or the governor, Felix (24:25–26). In short, Luke is consistent in endorsing generosity and hospitality throughout Acts, and in warning against the same greed that Jesus decried in his own ministry.

It would be an exaggeration to say, however, that we have sufficient evidence to show that all the protagonists of Acts "renounced all their possessions." For example, it would be insuperably speculative to try to discern whether, after conversion, Cornelius or Lydia dedicated all their possessions to the service of God and neighbor. But that lacuna in our knowledge does not represent a problem for Luke's wealth ethics. In all the places where we *can* identify Luke's approbation, we see him affirming as exemplary those who dedicate all to the kingdom.

While we might like to have more comment about the details of Cornelius's life or the nitty-gritty of the Antiochian Church, Luke does not offer us those details. After all, his ethical interests notwithstanding, Luke is doing a work of historiography, which means he does not have the freedom to invent historical details out of thin air. He has to use the traditions and information he has at hand, supporting his ethical agendas to whatever degrees he can without distorting the evidence to fit his agenda.

The fact of the matter is that the historian is constrained by his material. If Luke's research ended up showing that not all first-century believers did indeed renounce all their possessions as Luke's Jesus required, that did not mean that Luke's wealth ethics were thereby falsified; early Christians failed to obey Jesus in any number of ways. The disobedience of one's brother does not nullify one's own moral obligations!

The relevant point is that when Luke, as a historian, has a chance to continue to discuss wealth ethics in Acts, what he affirms and denies fits squarely with what we saw in the Gospel. He commends the thoroughgoing commitments of believers like Barnabas and Paul, who were radically generous; he applauds the Jerusalem community, which had *all* in common; and he severely censures people like Ananias and Sapphira, whose generosity fell short of committing the full proceeds from their field to the needs of the poor. While Luke no doubt recognized that not all early believers renounced all their possessions in service of the kingdom, he remains clear that precisely such a level of commitment *should be* forthcoming for those who claim to love God with all they are and have.

CONCLUSION

In Luke's second book, a history of the first decades of the Church, he remains committed to the subject of wealth ethics, even though he does not allot as much space to the subject as he does in the Gospel (when he had the opportunity to incorporate Jesus' extensive teachings on the subject of money). In his history, Luke has a new set of agendas, and while wealth ethics remains a priority, they are less central than in the Gospel. Furthermore, Luke is constrained by the material he has to work with: the actions of the imperfect people who comprised the early Church.

All those constraints notwithstanding, what Luke does affirm in Acts coheres with his wealth-ethical teachings in the Gospel. Faithful disciples of Jesus follow Jesus' teachings on generosity and hospitality. Those who are nonitinerant work hard to care for the traveling itinerants and for their poor, whether in their own communities (Acts 20:34–35) or in other cities (11:27–30). Indeed, they even at times divest themselves of wealth in order to succor a needy brother or sister (4:33–37).

Those figures whose behavior rises to the level of being paradigmatic are the members of the Jerusalem community, who have all in common; Barnabas, who divests himself to care for the poor; and Paul, who works a job while preaching in order to have funds to provide for the needs of his traveling companions and the poor in his community. The other paradigmatic figures are *negative* ones: Ananias and Sapphira exemplify what not to do, showing that being less than totally dedicated to the kingdom has dire consequences (5:1–11). God does not suffer idolaters lightly, and by holding back the proceeds of their field and lying about the matter, Ananias and Sapphira showed that they were also trying to serve mammon (Luke 16:13) and that they had not renounced all their possessions (Luke 14:33). So they were cast outside (Luke 14:35).

CHAPTER 6

Why Renounce All?

THROUGHOUT THIS BOOK, we have mostly been asking "*What* does Luke think about wealth ethics?" But in our discussion of Ananias and Sapphira in the previous chapter, we began to ask, "*Why* does Luke think what he thinks about wealth ethics?"

If we were reading other ancient books, we probably wouldn't invest too much energy trying to figure out the reasons for the author's extreme ethical positions. After all, city street corners and the blogosphere are densely populated with eccentric folk preaching ludicrous things about morality, and we give them the brush-off easily. But if you are reading Luke as a Christian, then you probably do not feel that you can just sweep aside his wealth ethics, even when he says something apparently ridiculous like "You can't be a disciple without renouncing all your possessions," or "It's right for God to smite someone who sells property to give to the church but then lies about the *percentage* of the proceeds donated." Luke's wealth ethics can seem extreme, which moves us from asking, "*What* does Luke think?" to "*Why* does Luke think that?"

Consequently, we will now examine the "theo-logic" of Luke's wealth ethics. The use of the hyphenated word *theo-logic* is not an attempt at cleverness; rather, the term intends to highlight the fact that the sort of logic that we see in the biblical texts is not identical with deductive logic or empirical science. Biblical authors construct arguments that are logical *given a set of beliefs* that are rooted in revelation, rather than in empirical verification. In other words, Luke does develop his ethics in a reasoned fashion, given his theological presuppositions. But if one doesn't share his theological presuppositions, then his ethics may not seem logical.[1]

This chapter will probe the reasons behind Luke's conviction that disciples should renounce all possessions as a ramification of their total commitment to love of God and love of neighbor (bearing in mind that "renouncing possessions" is really the negative way to say "dedicate all possessions to God"). In the process, we will see that Luke is especially motivated by these theological convictions: (1) love and mercy, (2) the Old Testament, (3) the dangers of wealth, (4) divine provision, and (5) eschatology. When you put these pieces together, you realize that, given Luke's theological beliefs, it would be hard to arrive at any other wealth ethic than the one elaborated in the previous chapters.

LOVE AND MERCY

We started our exploration of Luke's ethics with a discussion of the double love command (Luke 10:27) because the logic of the double love command is vital to understanding the extreme nature of Luke's wealth ethics. But once one grasps the very simple logic that one should love God "with all your heart, and with all your soul, and with all your strength (or "money," see ch. 3), and with all your mind," one realizes how hard it is to justify holding back money for selfish purposes. That's not to say that providing for one's physical needs is selfish; Acts 2:45 and 4:35 make it clear that *need* is precisely the criterion on which one should be giving to others—or by logical extension, keeping for oneself. Still, the word *need* gets bandied about in contemporary discourse (ever listen to people talk in a mall?) in a very different way from that used in biblical literature, which categorizes needs as food, clothing, and (sometimes) shelter.[2]

The logical extension of loving God with everything that one is and has is that one would love one's neighbor (whom God also loves). And so Luke pronounces that one must love one's neighbor *as oneself*. One could easily enough infer that this entails putting a neighbor's needs ahead of one's own wants, but Luke does not leave the matter up to inference. Luke's Jesus clarifies that what he means by "loving one's neighbor" is illustrated by the behavior of the Good Samaritan, who became a neighbor to someone who was not his neighbor by showing him mercy: risking his own safety and spending his own money to help the half-dead stranger (10:30–37). This is our example, our paradigm, insofar as we are told (with the scribe to whom Jesus spoke), "Go and do likewise." Unless one anticipates that in the future one will no longer have (potential) neighbors in need, the necessity to renounce all possessions will remain poignant.

The Sermon on the Plain hones the point by explaining that, in loving our neighbor by showing mercy, we imitate God: "Be merciful, just as your Father is merciful" (6:36). In fact, the context of that verse focuses on loving enemies, giving generously, and lending with no expectation of recovering your investment (6:29–35). In the Sermon on the Plain, as in Luke 10, the Evangelist excludes the possibility of restricting the definition of those to whom we are to show mercy; he even specifies that the obligation to practice mercy extends to one's *enemies*. Luke also leaves no room to doubt that the aforementioned mercy should be shown financially. Jesus calls his disciples to imitate the God who has shown them great mercy by likewise showing mercy, even "to the ungrateful and the wicked" (6:35).

In other words, Luke's Jesus expects his followers to love God with all they have and to love their neighbors as themselves by showing anyone to whom they can become a neighbor the sort of mercy that God has shown them. In that light, it becomes quite obvious why Jesus would say, "None of you can become my disciple if you do not give up all your possessions" (14:33). What other option would be viable?

THE OLD TESTAMENT

Jesus did not fabricate the double love command from whole cloth; rather, he stitched it together from two key Old Testament texts: Deuteronomy 6:5 and Leviticus 19:18. Jesus understood his ethics to be rooted in the Old Testament; in other words, he was teaching his disciples how to keep the Law (or at least how to keep what he understood to be the most essential messages of the Law).

RENOUNCING EVERYTHING

Indeed, Jesus understood his own mission and wealth ethics to be very much in continuity with the Law.

For example, Jesus' public "debut" in Luke's Gospel consists of him reading from the Book of Isaiah (a combination of Isa 61:1–3 and 58:6–7), saying,

> "The Spirit of the Lord is upon me,
> because *he has anointed me to bring good news to
> the poor.*
> He has sent me to proclaim release to the captives
> and recovery of sight to the blind, to let the
> oppressed go free,
> to proclaim the year of the Lord's favor."...
> Then he began to say to them, "Today this scripture has been fulfilled in your hearing." (4:18–19, 21, emphasis mine)

In other words, when Jesus cared for the marginalized and taught his disciples to do the same, he did so because that is what the Old Testament said he, as the Messiah, was supposed to do. His wealth ethics are inextricably integrated in the teaching and prophecies of the Old Testament.

This conviction comes to the fore again when Jesus reams out the Pharisees and scribes in Luke 11:37–52. He launches into his denunciation by saying,

> Now you Pharisees clean the outside of the cup and of the dish, but inside you are full of greed and wickedness. You fools! Did not the one who made the outside make the inside also? So *give alms with respect to that which is within*,[3] and behold, everything will be clean for you. But woe to you Pharisees! For you tithe mint and rue and herbs of all kinds, and *neglect justice and the love of God*; it is these you ought to have practiced, without neglecting the others. (11:39–42, NRSV with modifications by author).

Jesus' invective against the Pharisees focuses on the way they gave fastidious attention to elements of the Law and the oral

Why Renounce All?

traditions that were of secondary importance (purity laws and tithing) while neglecting the most essential features of the Law: caring for the poor, practicing justice, and loving God.[4] Rather than thinking that washing dishes would make them pure, Jesus says that caring for the poor ("giving alms") will make them internally pure (Dan 4:27; Prov 15:27 [LXX]; Sir 3:30; cf. 1 Tim 6:18–19).[5] The accusation that the Pharisees "neglect justice and the love of God" (Luke 11:42) alludes to the Old Testament; Jesus, here, invokes Micah 6:8, which explains that what is good and what the Lord requires is to "do justice, and to love kindness." Consequently, Jesus' ethical teachings are an expression of what he considers the top priorities of the Old Testament.[6]

The parable of the rich man and Lazarus (16:19–31) illustrates this point rather more graphically. In that story, the rich man is sent to Hades to be tormented after a lifetime of having failed to feed and clothe his neighbor, Lazarus. He calls out to Abraham, begging that Lazarus might be sent back to warn his brothers (who presumably were living a similarly egoistic existence), but Abraham replies, "They have Moses and the prophets; they should listen to them" (16:29; cf. 16:31).

The interesting (though often overlooked) question is, Why does Abraham mention "Moses and the Prophets," that is, the Old Testament? He does so, ostensibly, because the Old Testament teaches something that the rich man failed to do, as a result of which he landed in torment. But which part of the Old Testament could be in view? One only has to look at the way that Luke invokes the Old Testament to know what he has in mind:

- Love your neighbor as yourself (Lev 19:18, cited in Luke 10:27),
- Proclaim good news to the poor (Isa 61:1, cited in Luke 4:18),
- Show mercy to those in need (Mic 6:8, alluded to in Luke 11:41).

Indeed, the very details of the present parable call to mind Isaiah 58:6–7 (cited in Luke 4:18), insofar as the rich man failed to do for Lazarus precisely the things that Isaiah tells Israel to do:

> Is not this the fast that I choose:...
> to share your bread with the hungry,
>   and bring the homeless poor into your house;
> when you see the naked, to cover them,
>   and not to hide yourself from your own kin?

In other words, when Abraham tells the rich man that he should have listened to Moses and the prophets, he reveals, once again, that Luke's wealth ethics are founded on the commandments of the Old Testament. By following Jesus' teachings on wealth, Luke implies that one obeys God's will as revealed in the Law.

THE DANGERS OF WEALTH

Nonetheless, renunciation of possessions is not just about caring for the poor; it is also about guarding *one's own soul*. Luke is keenly aware of how dangerous wealth can be for one's salvation, insofar as it so frequently thwarts those who might otherwise want to follow Jesus' path of self-sacrificial love. (Naturally, if you're trapped in poverty, what do you have to lose by following Jesus? But if you have a villa and a vineyard and a retinue of servants, you might be less enthusiastic to go slum it with an eccentric rabbi.) Consider, in this vein, the parable of the soils. Jesus says that the seed that fell among thorns, germinated, and then was choked out (8:7) represents "the ones who hear; but as they go on their way, they are choked by *the cares and riches and pleasures of life*, and their fruit does not mature" (8:14, emphasis mine). In short, Jesus warns that money and pleasures can strangle discipleship and forestall fruitfulness.

As we noted earlier, Luke states his case even more emphatically in Jesus' encounter with the rich ruler. When the affluent man is saddened by Jesus' demand that he divest himself of riches, Jesus comments,

> How hard it is for those who have wealth to enter the kingdom of God! Indeed, it is easier for a camel to go through the eye of a needle than for someone who is rich to enter the kingdom of God. (18:24–25)

Why Renounce All?

Interpreters over the years have rather willfully tried to soften this maxim (claiming that the word translated "camel" really means "rope" or that there was a first-century gate in Jerusalem called "the eye of the needle," neither of which are true). But Jesus' point is hardly subtle: just as it is quite thoroughly impossible for a camel to go through a needle's eye, so also is it quite impossible for a rich man to enter the kingdom of God. And in case the imagery doesn't make the point starkly enough, Jesus elaborates that it is, for all intents and purposes, a divine *miracle* when rich people are saved: "What is impossible for mortals is possible for God" (18:27).

This comparison is another example of *hyperbole* (overstatement). Jesus is exaggerating for effect, as we can see from the fact that Luke does describe *some* rich people in positive terms (like Zacchaeus in 19:1–10 or Joseph of Arimathea in 23:50–53). But, as was emphasized in chapter 3, the whole point of hyperbole is to make it clear that the matter in question is *important*. For Luke, this issue is deadly serious. Riches are such an obstacle to discipleship that the Sermon on the Plain mourns, "Woe to you who are rich, for you have received your consolation" (6:24), and by contrast blesses the poor who possess the kingdom of God (6:20). So also, Luke fills his Gospel with stories of ill-fated rich people (the rich fool of 12:16–20; the rich guests of 14:15–24; the rich man of 16:19–31), not in order to malign the rich, but to admonish the well-heeled that their wealth imperils their discipleship. This is yet another reason why Jesus unflinchingly warns people that they cannot be disciples unless they renounce their possessions.

DIVINE PROVISION

The problem is that, if you renounce your possessions, you become vulnerable. Money provides a safety net, a sense of security. Luke realized that he would need to address his readers' concerns about physical survival in order to convince many people to renounce their possessions in order to follow Jesus. Thus, Luke emphasized that God will take care of those who follow Jesus, just

RENOUNCING EVERYTHING

as God provides for all the idle creatures of the earth, such as the raven and the lily.

> Do not worry about your life, what you will eat, or about your body, what you will wear....Consider the ravens: they neither sow nor reap, they have neither storehouse nor barn, and yet God feeds them. Of how much more value are you than the birds!...Consider the lilies, how they grow: they neither toil nor spin; yet I tell you, even Solomon in all his glory was not clothed like one of these. But if God so clothes the grass of the field, which is alive today and tomorrow is thrown into the oven, how much more will he clothe you—you of little faith! And do not keep striving for what you are to eat and what you are to drink, and do not keep worrying. For it is the nations of the world that strive after all these things, and your Father knows that you need them. Instead, strive for his kingdom, and these things will be given to you as well. (Luke 12:22, 24, 27–31)

Jesus assures his audience that God is aware of their needs, and that, if they seek the kingdom, those needs will be met.

Notice, however, the way that Luke has adjusted his source text in 12:30. Whereas Matthew 6:33 says, "But strive first for the kingdom of God and his righteousness, and *all* these things will be given to you as well," Luke removes a key word: *all*. Normally, Luke adds the word *all* to his sources (as we saw in 5:11, 28; 18:22), but here Luke *drops* the word *all*! Why? In order to make it clear that the things God will "add" to the disciples are just the necessities of life (12:30) mentioned in this same discourse: food and clothing (12:23). In this way, Luke heads off those who would attempt to twist Jesus' words into a promise of riches and ease. God will clothe and feed his emissaries, Luke says, even as the disciples follow the Son of Man who has nowhere to lay his head.

As noted in chapter 4, Luke illustrates the reliability of God's provision for Jesus' disciples in the itinerancy instructions of 9:1–6 and 10:1–11. The Twelve and the Seventy go out to preach without provisions, with nothing more than the clothes on their back. And yet, in spite of being as vulnerable as "lambs into the midst

Why Renounce All?

of wolves" (10:3), God provides for them and they never lack for anything (22:35). Thus, the itinerants' experiences and the teachings of Luke 12 answer the reasonable and prudent objections that arise in reaction to Luke 14:33; God can be trusted to provide for those who renounce all their possessions to follow Jesus.

ESCHATOLOGY

We have seen a number of the theological pillars that support Luke's wealth ethics, but the doctrine to which Luke appeals with greatest frequency is that of *eschatological recompense*. (This is just a theological way of saying that in the end, the good guys will get rewarded and the bad guys will get punished.) If you trace the development of the Old Testament, starting with the earlier books and moving toward the later ones, there is an increasing awareness of the injustice of the present life. Solomon may have felt comfortable saying that the poor are in need because they are lazy and impious, while the rich owe their good fortune to hard work and godly living;[7] he was a rich king, after all! But, by the time the exile rolled around and the Israelite people had lost their family farms to godless pagans, the wisdom of Proverbs may have seemed inadequate. As a result, the later Old Testament authors point toward the afterlife as the time when the wicked will be punished and the just will be rewarded, even though the wicked often prospered in this life while the righteous often suffered.[8] Scholars refer to this idea of future punishment and reward as "reversal of fortunes" or "eschatological reversal," and the theme occurs all over Luke's Gospel.[9]

Early in Luke's Gospel, Mary gives voice to quite conventional expectations of eschatological reversal; she expresses her belief that the Messiah will reverse the fortunes of the poor and pious Jews and the rich and wicked Romans (1:52–53). But as the book unfolds, Luke shifts the emphasis and points out that the reversal of fortunes will not transpire along ethnic lines, such that the Jews can smugly await the castigation of the Romans (2:34; 3:7–14). On the contrary, Jesus foretells a reversal *within* Israel, an inversion of the fortunes of the rich and the poor, the social insiders and the marginalized. That's why the Sermon on the Plain pronounces, "Blessed are you who are poor, for yours is the kingdom of God....But woe to you who are rich, for you have received your consolation" (6:20, 24). That's also partly why, in Luke 16:19–31, the rich man is tormented in Hades while Lazarus is comforted at Abraham's bosom: "Child, remember that during your lifetime you received your good things, and Lazarus in like manner evil things; but now he is comforted here, and you are in agony" (16:25). Such bold rhetoric certainly underscores the dangers of wealth!

This raises the following question: If one is to expect an eschatological reversal, what can the rich do to escape their fate? Jesus' answer is both clear and logical: to avoid damnation, the rich should serve those who are currently suffering and who will ultimately benefit from the eschatological reversal.

Banquet Teachings

This idea is illustrated nicely in the banquet teachings of Luke 14:1–24, a text that turns on the typical social dynamics of ancient banquets. Banquets were often self-aggrandizing affairs, in which the host could show off his wealth and also curry the loyalty of his important friends and clients. Where one sat at a banquet reflected one's social status; those reclining closer to the host were the VIPs and would often receive better food and wine, as a way of demarking their superior status. Given the way that banquets were venues in which to jockey for social position, one can appreciate that such events were normally put on for important people, not for the poor or the marginalized. After all, poor people were at the bottom of the social hierarchy; moreover, one could only expect to receive a reciprocal benefit for one's generosity from someone with something to give (but cf. 6:32–35).

When Jesus attends a banquet hosted by a leading Pharisee, however, he decries the typical hustle for seats of honor (14:8–11) as well as the fact that the Pharisee had chosen (per standard custom) to invite only important people and his own family members (14:12). Reversing customary practice, Jesus tells the host that, next time he puts on a shindig, he should invite "the poor, the crippled, the lame, and the blind" (14:13)—because their inability

Why Renounce All?

to return the favor means that "you will be repaid at the resurrection of the righteous" (14:14).

Basically, the idea is that generosity to poor people (whom God loves and protects[10]) puts God in one's debt, as Proverbs 19:17 says: "Whoever is kind to the poor lends to the Lord, and will be repaid in full." How will God repay? Jesus answers that the recompense will come at the resurrection.

Jesus' indelicate dinner-table conversation makes the guests uncomfortable, so one of them chimes in with a smarmy spiritual truism: "Blessed is anyone who will eat bread in the kingdom of God!" (14:15). At that, Jesus whips around and tells a parable that warns his fellow diners that, in spite of their self-assurance, they should not be expecting that they will pull up a chair at the eschatological banquet. To make this point, Jesus elaborates a parable about the people who can and cannot expect to dine in God's kingdom. He describes three different people who were invited to the banquet (the characters in the parable are transparent stand-ins for those sitting around the table with Jesus). Each of those invited declines the invitation, because they have better things to do.

The first guest begs off because he has just bought a piece of land; the second sends his apologies because he has just acquired five yoke of oxen. These purchases make one thing clear: both of those characters are rich. In an agrarian society comprised mostly of peasant farmers who inherit their land from their parents, only the affluent can save enough capital to purchase a new piece of land. Likewise, five yoke of oxen are able to plow around a hundred acres, whereas a peasant farmer typically only had a parcel of five or six acres. The fact that these rich men decide not to come to the banquet because they are too preoccupied with their recent purchases sharply underscores Luke's concerns about the dangers of wealth.

The host of the fictional banquet (an obvious cipher for God) is incensed by the effrontery of his guests, and so he sends for "the poor, the crippled, the blind, and the lame" (14:21)—that is, the same people Jesus told his own host, the Pharisee, to invite to his next banquet. The host of the parable declares that none of the other ingrates he had originally invited would taste his dinner (14:24). In the parabolic scenario, it seems like the host is pouting; but when one bears in mind that the host represents God and the dinner represents the eschatological celebration in the kingdom, verse 24 becomes a great deal more ominous. The basic message is that rich people, like those sitting at the table with Jesus, may find themselves in hell, unless they start caring for the people who would never otherwise be invited to dine with them—the people that Jesus himself served (cf. 4:18; 6:20–23; 7:22).

The Unjust Steward

The same strategy for avoiding eschatological punishment is proposed in the parable of the unjust steward (16:1–9). That parable describes a steward who is about to get fired and needs to find himself a cushy new job, knowing that he can't make it as a beggar or a blue-collar worker (16:1–4). So the steward uses the possessions that are under his control (even though they are not his own property) to reduce the debts of his bosses' rich clients significantly. Each of the debtors receives a debt reduction of about five hundred denarii, which is a significant sum, given that a denarius is a day's wage for normal peasant laborer (16:5–8). In return for being the agent of this big windfall, the steward hopes that one of these two clients (they are probably merchants) will give him a job after he is fired.

The social dynamics of this parable are vexing for modern readers,[11] but Jesus' interpretation is not hard to understand, given his theo-logic. "And I tell you, make friends for yourselves by means of dishonest wealth so that when it is gone, they may welcome you into the eternal homes" (16:9). Jesus' basic idea is that his listeners should use their earthly riches ("dishonest wealth")—which in truth belong to God and not to them (see 16:11–12)—in order to gain access to eternal life. But, in a striking departure from social convention, the people who should receive their generosity are not other rich people (like the clients of 16:5–7). On the contrary, Jesus tells his listeners to give to the people who will be in a position to "welcome them into the eternal homes," that is, *the poor, for theirs is the kingdom of God* (see 6:20) *and they are the ones who will eat of the eschatological banquet* (14:21–24).[12]

In other words, by helping the poor, the rich get on the good side of God (14:14) and of the poor, who are themselves already on God's good side. Luke explains that the way to avoid being on

Why Renounce All?

the wrong side of the eschatological reversal is by siding with those who will be on the right side: the poor and the needy.

CONCLUSION

When you see the big picture from Luke's theological point of view, it becomes obvious why he thinks that disciples of Jesus have to renounce all of their possessions (14:33) and dedicate them to the work of the kingdom. Let's now bring all the pieces together.

Disciples of Jesus must love God with all they have and are, and they must love their neighbors as themselves (10:27) (*Love and Mercy*). Insofar as one will never run out of needy people to whom one can become a neighbor, there is little room to justify keeping superfluous wealth for oneself rather than showing mercy to a neighbor in dire need.

On the flip side, holding onto extra wealth puts one in spiritual peril (8:14; 18:24–25), insofar as riches are dangerous temptations to shy away from the sacrifices of being Jesus' disciple (*The Dangers of Wealth*). Luke anticipates that his readers who renounce all will be concerned about their own survival, but assures them the same God who cares for the creation will care for them (12:22–31; cf. 9:1–6; 10:1–11) (*Divine Provision*).

Luke further reinforces his case by pointing out that the Law itself has always demanded care for the poor and needy (4:18–19; 10:27; 11:37–42; 16:29–30) (*The Old Testament*). But, in caring for such people, one can expect eschatological reward, since God will repay what the poor cannot (14:14). Indeed, if one is rich, Luke argues that it is *only* by renouncing one's possessions and caring for the poor that one can hope to escape the punishment to come upon those who have defied the Law by neglecting their brothers and sisters in need (14:16–24; 16:1–9, 19–31; 18:22). If one doesn't seek justice and mercy now, one can be assured of receiving justice, but not mercy, in the life to come (16:25) (*Eschatology*).

Luke's case for the necessity of total dedication of one's wealth to the kingdom of God is a strong one. It reflects the teachings of Jesus and it is sustained by a powerful theo-logic, compelling reasoning based on Luke's beliefs about God's character and operation in this world and the next.

And that's all well and good. Unless you are, like me, a rich person (at least relative to the majority of the world's population) reading the New Testament in the twenty-first century, and wanting to be Jesus' disciple, but really not wanting to renounce all possessions.

CHAPTER 7

Guidance for the Contemporary Disciple

ONE OF OUR GOALS THROUGHOUT this book has been to "Let Luke be Luke" (see chapter 2), to let the Gospel author say whatever he wants to say without hedging against the uncomfortable ramifications that his idealistic wealth ethics might have for those who read the Gospels as Scripture. Still, most readers will not be driven by detached intellectual curiosity about the ideology of a first-century doctor-turned-biographer. So how does one take Luke seriously, while also taking seriously the fact that Luke never anticipated that Christianity would become the world's largest religious movement on a globe with several billion people, a large percentage of which lives in poverty? How does one take his Gospel's wealth ethics as Scripture—realizing that Luke would have held a zero-sum, agrarian view of economics—while we today live in a society sustained (and driven) by wealth creation on a global scale? What can Luke tell us that is relevant for twenty-first-century Christianity, and what can't he tell us?

WHAT LUKE CAN TELL US

Notwithstanding all the differences between Luke's world and ours, if one counts oneself as a disciple of Jesus, Luke can give us at very least three key things: a goal, a preliminary hierarchy, and a preliminary theology of vocation. (This list is intentionally lean and in no way pretends to be comprehensive.)

A Goal: Committing Everything to God

There is no reason to think that the double love command (Luke 10:27) should not continue to frame the Christian moral vision. The notion that we should seek the kingdom of God (12:31), particularly in loving our neighbor, is not bound by culture or time, even if the *ways* of doing that will certainly be influenced by culture. By extension, the exhortation for disciples to renounce all their possessions should also be a timeless imperative for Christians, since that renunciation is the logical ramification of total dedication to God and of loving of one's neighbor as oneself.

The negative formulation of Luke 14:33, emphasizing "renunciation" rather than "giving," reflects Jesus' earnest warnings about the dangers of wealth (see chapter 6). Nonetheless, given that the renunciation is prescribed *for the purpose* of loving God and loving one's neighbor, it might be apt to reformulate Luke 14:33 in positive terms, in order to provide a more all-encompassing summation of Luke's wealth ethics. Thus, we might say, "Every disciple of Jesus must *commit all* of his or her resources to the kingdom."[1]

The key feature of this formulation is the *thoroughgoing character* of the dedication of the resources; the same notion appears in the account of the widow's mite (Luke 21:1–4; see chapter 4). The basic thesis of the story is that God evaluates one's generosity not on how much one gives, but on how much one keeps for oneself. Totality of investment is contiguous with totality of love, whereas mediocrity of investment reflects a tepidity of affection. Where your treasure is, there your heart will be also (Luke 12:34).

This is the wealth-ethical goal of the disciple of Jesus in any day: to dedicate all his or her resources to the kingdom of God. Nonetheless, we saw in the narratives of Luke and Acts that renunciation takes a variety of forms; so likewise, we should expect that contemporary renunciation will exhibit a similar or even greater degree of diversity. When we look at the narratives of Luke and Acts, for example, we see that disciples are affirmed for diverse expressions of renunciation: leaving behind most everything, like the Twelve did (though not being totally indigent; see Luke 22:33–35); divesting oneself completely, unlike the rich ruler (18:18–30); balancing divestiture and restitution for past wrongs, as Zacchaeus did (19:1–10); spending progressively and generously to support those who have abandoned or divested themselves of possessions, as Mary, Susanna, and Joanna did (Luke 8:1–13); selling off possessions and sharing daily life to support the needy in one's community (Acts 2:42–47; 4:32–35); working diligently to provide for one's own needs,[2] the needs of one's friends, and the needs of the poor in one's community, like Paul did (Acts 20:34–35). Luke does not have a single model of renunciation, and it is not always exhaustive, but it is always profound: a serious and sacrificial dedication of all one's goods to the work of God and the love of neighbor.

The Double Love Command

Beyond giving us a goal, Luke provides the beginning of a *hierarchy* with which to think about ordering one's use of possessions. In a vertical sense, Luke helps us think about how to prioritize certain decisions over others. The double love command shows that, even though the love of neighbor is intimately connected to the love of God, the love of God is not exhausted in the love of neighbor, nor is it of equal importance to the love of neighbor. Notice that the command to love God "with all your heart, and with all your soul, and with all your strength, and with all your mind" essentially entails loving God more than one loves oneself—which is why it follows that one would "hate…even life itself," carry one's cross, and lose one's life following Jesus (14:26–27). By contrast, the command to love one's neighbor as oneself means loving one's neighbor *less than* God. So there is a *prioritization* of loving God over loving one's neighbor, even though there is *not a contrast* between loving God and loving one's neighbor.

This prioritization indicates that it may be legitimate to make expenditures for the work of God that do not have immediate humanitarian payoff. Jesus praises the widow for casting the last of her money into the temple treasury (Luke 21:1–4), and those funds went to support the temple worship, not to sustain the needy. Although Jesus excoriates the Pharisees for their failure to care for the poor, he still affirms that they should continue tithing (Luke 11:42); first tithes, however, supported the cult and the Levites, rather than the indigent, the widow, and the orphans.[3] So one can justify directing wealth toward "the love of God" even if it does not redound immediately in the "love of neighbor," though one does struggle to think of actions expressing love of God that do not by extension end up blessing one's neighbor.

It would be wrong to read this last paragraph as driving a wedge between spiritual and humanitarian work, or justifying the neglect of the vulnerable on the basis of one's commitment to the work of the Church. Such a dichotomy must be resisted, and in the diversity of our expenditures, the person who loves God and neighbor should attend to both parties, recognizing that in loving the neighbor, they also love the God who loves their neighbor too (see chapter 3).

Vocational Diversity

This preliminary vertical hierarchy can be complemented by a preliminary horizontal hierarchy. While all disciples of Jesus will share the commitment to loving God first and to loving neighbor as oneself, the ways in which that love is expressed will differ from disciple to disciple, depending on their vocational diversity.

The *bi-vocational* explanation recognized already that followers of Jesus fall broadly into two categories in Luke's Gospel: the itinerant and nonitinerant. This basic distinction in vocations has ramifications for *how* the respective groups renounce all for the kingdom, although the examples of Zacchaeus and the poor widow make it clear that total dedication *remains incumbent* upon the nonitinerant. This bi-vocational schema reflects the dynamics of the Jesus movement during his lifetime; Luke also shows how both vocations complement one another, as the nonitinerants enable the ministry of the itinerants through generous hospitality. But the Book of Acts already begins to nuance the binary schema, as the Twelve settle down in Jerusalem—following their itinerancy with Jesus—and as Paul alternates between itinerancy and nonitinerancy, in Corinth and Ephesus. All this anticipates the more robust Pauline schema of a single body with

Guidance for the Contemporary Disciple

many parts, all of which contribute optimally to the body *in their diversity* (1 Cor 12:4–31).

The bi-vocational explanation of Luke's Gospel, however, is only a preliminary division; Luke's narrative fans those two basic lifestyles out into several expressions of wealth ethics. Peter and the rich ruler and Joanna are all called to itinerancy, but that common vocation does not change the fact that their renunciation took different forms: Peter abandoning all, the ruler selling his possessions, Joanna bankrolling Jesus and the Twelve. These distinct forms of renunciation reflect the fact that they had different amounts of money to begin with and also that their life circumstances differed. The same can be said of the nonitinerants. Zacchaeus's past history and relative wealth entail that he commits all to the kingdom in a way that is different from the widow in Luke 20 or from the Jerusalem Christians in Acts 2 and 4.

The *personalist* explanation thus appreciates that there are unique contours to the wealth ethics of the characters in Luke and Acts, even though those unique contours should all be seen as expressions of total commitment to the kingdom. In this way, one can draw a wealth-ethical analogy to Paul's image of the Church's body being one with many parts: just as Christians have a wide diversity of callings to service to the kingdom, so also it is right that they should dedicate all their possessions to that kingdom in a wide variety of ways.

These observations fit well with what we know about the ancient biographical and historiographical genres. Both those genres capitalized on exemplary figures to flesh out what a given philosophical or moral teaching means; what it might look like in practice. This suggests that the only generically sensitive and hermeneutically responsible way to interpret Luke's wealth ethics is with an eye to the actions of his characters. The diversity of those characters' actions reveals that there are many right ways to dedicate one's possessions to the kingdom, and that it would be wrong to force every disciple into one of two molds.

This personalist emphasis does not, however, mean that "anything goes," that there is "no wrong way" to renounce all! Renouncing possessions is not like eating a Reese's Peanut Butter Cup. Quite the contrary, Luke 14:33 sets a high bar, even if we take hyperbole and narrative diversity into account. Ananias and Sapphira were *wrong* to divest themselves of a field but lie about giving all the proceeds to the apostles. The rich fool (Luke 12:15–21) was wrong to have stored up his great harvest in barns; the Pharisees were wrong to tithe carefully but to neglect almsgiving (11:37–42). Those with two tunics would be wrong not to share with their neighbor who has none (3:11); it would have been wrong, too, if Zacchaeus had only given his possessions to the poor but hadn't made restitution for his extortion. There is a great gulf between a monolithic morality and ethical relativism. Put differently, just because Luke doesn't give us a "one-size-fits-all" ethic, it does *not* mean that anything goes.

In the twenty-first century, Christian vocations will differ in many ways from those of the first century. (Indeed, the vocations in the time of Paul already differed from the vocations in the time of Jesus.) Those distinct vocations will inform the ways in which twenty-first-century disciples renounce all possessions, as will the diverse and unique life circumstances of the contemporary disciple. In this diversity, however, the wealth ethics of one disciple can complement the wealth ethics of another disciple, as was the case for the symbiosis between the itinerant and nonitinerant disciples during Jesus' and Paul's ministries. Nonetheless, all this diversity of legitimate wealth ethics notwithstanding, the Church has a prophetic obligation to articulate that the vast majority of our contemporary practices in the North Atlantic certainly cannot be characterized as dedicating all to the kingdom or loving our neighbors as ourselves.

WHAT LUKE CAN'T TELL US

It is of no small moral value to have a wealth-ethical goal—dedication of all to the kingdom—and to have some preliminary ways to organize and think through how to realize that goal in different circumstances—recognizing the supremacy of love of God even over love of neighbor; appreciating the diversity of ways in which distinct people in distinct vocations realize their renunciation of all in service of discipleship. But this does not change the fact that a great deal more needs to be said before we arrive at anything like a satisfying twenty-first-century wealth ethic.

In the first place, Luke can't tell *you* how you should dedicate your all to the kingdom. It would be no more appropriate for us to imagine that the third Gospel has precisely the formula for a specific reader's renunciation today than it would be to prescribe Zacchaeus's form of renunciation to Mary Magdalene. The vocation of the contemporary reader and her unique life circumstances render it rather silly to imagine that Luke's text is capable of determining how she specifically should dedicate all to the kingdom. Luke's diverse forms of renunciation are not an exhaustive list; they are specific instantiations of renunciation of all that should help inspire later readers to find a way to practice similar integrity, generosity, and sacrificial love in their own unique calling and circumstances.

This leads us to our second point: Luke can't tell us how *best* to love the needy in the twenty-first century. Luke does not even implicitly indicate that the forms of generosity he narrates would be apt for a different century, let alone a different millennium. In Luke and Acts, almsgiving and divestiture are among the primary ways that disciples care for the poor. While one need not exclude these measures from a portfolio of ways that we can help those who are suffering today, modern economic knowledge might suggest that we decenter almsgiving and divestiture as ways to aid the vulnerable. It is arguable that selling off a productive field in an agrarian economy (cf. Barnabas, Ananias, and Sapphira) was not the most financially savvy decision possible; one could well suggest that Ananias's field could have had a great long-term benefit if he allowed the poor in his community to work it rent free and keep all the net income for themselves. Almsgiving (i.e., charitable donations) does sometimes foster relations of dependence between the donor and the recipient, whereas one sees large-scale and long-term welfare gains through charitable microfinance (such as that practiced by Opportunity International) that couples interest-free loans with vocational training for people with a viable business plan. It does not seem that these possibilities were on early Christianity's radar.[4] Moreover, there are now people—such as Dr. Toby Ord, founder of the organization Giving What We Can[5]—doing serious statistical research calculating what sorts of charitable giving will have the maximum impact on people's well-being, measured in terms of "Quality Adjusted Life Years."[6] This is far more sophisticated than any reflection we see in the early Church, but there is no reason to think that the advances in social-scientific knowledge should not be applied to Christian wealth ethics. Indeed, failing to do so probably constitutes a failure to "Love the Lord your God…with all your *mind*" (Luke 10:27, emphasis mine).

So, even though Luke can tell us a great deal about Christian wealth ethics, his Gospel does not tell you personally how to renounce all, nor does it tell us how we can best love our neighbors today. Those things we have to figure out for ourselves, in cooperation with the Holy Spirit.

NEXT STEPS FOR ADOPTING LUKE'S WEALTH ETHICS

A proper practical guide to Christian wealth ethics will require another book, but perhaps it would not be inappropriate to offer a few preliminary suggestions for individuals who want to pursue the sort of discipleship described by Luke.

Repentance

Although this may seem out of place for an academic book, it should be relatively obvious from what we have read thus far that very few people actually live in the way that Luke enjoins. The fact that the essential imperative of the Gospel is to love God with all of one's being, with all that one has, and that one is to love one's neighbor as oneself, makes this glaringly obvious. Nobody does that! Yet, if you are a Christian, this is the goal, the way that we would be if we could, the way that we will be when God's will is done on earth as it is in heaven. But in the present, we remain hamstrung by egotism, selfishness, and woundedness, all of which limit our ability to love. For that reason, repentance is a central theme of Luke, as it is for the rest of the Synoptic Gospels.

John the Baptist's ministry is described as preparing the way of the Lord (Luke 3:4). But he prepared the way *by calling Israel to repentance* (3:3). And when the crowds of people seeking his baptism of repentance were so numerous that John doubted their earnestness ("You brood of vipers" [3:7]), he warned them that they would need to "*bear fruits* worthy of repentance" (3:8), rather than counting on his baptism and "Abraham our ancestor" to save them. The crowds pressed him for specificity: "What then should we do?" (3:10); John replied with wealth ethics: they should share their food and clothing with the needy, and those in authority (soldiers and tax collectors) should cease to abuse their power for their own self-enrichment (3:11–14).

John the Baptist's wealth ethics is by no means as developed as that of Jesus or Luke—he was, after all, only *preparing* the way—but John teaches us, from the beginning of Luke's Gospel, that wealth ethics *proceeds from* repentance. Wealth ethics does not justify or save, but follows repentance, as "fruits worthy of repentance" (3:8).

So we begin with, and return to, repentance: for not loving our neighbor as ourselves, for seeking security in superfluous wealth, for spending on trifles like digital music, and for drinking pour-over coffees when Lazarus lies outside our gates, hungry and covered in sores. We repent because we want to love our neighbor; we repent because we believe that "even now the ax is lying at the root of the trees; every tree therefore that does not bear good fruit is cut down and thrown into the fire" (3:9). A Christian life that is not initiated and sustained by repentance from sin is an exercise in self-delusion.

Restoration

Repentance is not, however, simply an exercise in apology to God, let alone a discipline of self-loathing. Repentance, more aptly, consists of acknowledging one's spiritual malaise and the submission to treatment by the soul's physician. However strident Luke's warnings against greed may be, poignant stories of repentance and healing also wind their way through the wealth-ethical teachings of his Gospel. And those who manifest the most lavish generosity toward Christ and their neighbors are quite often the forgiven sinners whom Jesus has healed.

No text of the Gospels displays the experience of spiritual and psychological healing with such raw and emotional candor as the account of Jesus' anointing by the sinful woman (Luke 7:36–50). Her utter abandon, her self-forgetful tears of relief, her weeping prostration at Jesus' feet, all generate a moment of unmistakable recognition for those who have themselves experienced God's emotional healing. In her overwhelming joy, gratitude, and love, she sloshes perfume of great value onto the feet of her healer, delighting to pour out her wealth to honor Jesus. And Jesus does not fail to connect this extravagant gift with her repentance and healing: "Her sins, which were many, have been forgiven; hence she has shown great love" (7:47).

In fact, Luke's Gospel includes numerous texts that connect repentance, healing, and generosity. Levi, the sinful tax collector who left all to be Jesus' disciple, is said to have been "sick," in need of Jesus' healing (5:31–32). The tax collectors, as collaborators with the Roman Empire, suffered the daily judgments and loathing of their communities; that social stigma must have bored its way into their sense of self, into their hearts. But the parable of the prodigal son (15:11–32), undoubtedly Jesus' most moving tale of restoration between God and his iniquitous people, is told precisely in response to the timid overtures toward repentance being made by publicans and sinners (15:1). The reconciliation of sinful tax collectors is described in terms no less poignant than a father recklessly embracing and effusively celebrating the homecoming of his lost child.

How do these restored sinners react to such love? They respond with generosity. Zacchaeus and Levi throw great banquets for Jesus. Thereafter, Levi leaves everything behind to be Jesus' disciple while Zacchaeus channels all of his affluence toward righting his wrongs and aiding the needy. Things are much the same in the case of the women disciples who provide for Jesus and the Twelve (8:3). Joanna, Mary, and Susanna had been cured of their sicknesses and freed of their demons (8:2). It was as a result of that healing that they then dedicated their resources to the kingdom of God. The thoroughgoing renunciation and abundant liberality of the infirmed, the outcast, the oppressed, are intimately interwoven with their healing and restoration.

It should not strike us as odd, then, to note that the bracing injunctions to generosity in the Sermon on the Plain (Luke 6:30–31, 33–34, 38) are interlaced with teachings on love (6:23), the mercy of God the Father (6:35–36), and the suspension of judgment and condemnation (6:37). Luke understands that love begets love. By contrast, selfish greed and self-aggrandizing benefaction (cf. 22:25) can both be manifestations of hidden spiritual woundedness, and it is futile to treat the symptoms of egotism without healing the underlying infection.

This means that repentance for sins of greed should not terminate merely in a resolution to be more munificent. Such repentance ought to be a prelude to seeking healing, transformation, and restoration, trusting that God will make us what we were meant to be. Generous and joyous dedication of all one's possessions to the kingdom is inspired by love, not guilt.

Vocation

The next step for those seeking to bear fruits worthy of repentance is to reflect on their calling. It is probably one's professional vocation, the work to which one is called, that will give the dominant shape to how it is that one loves God with all that one has and is. The career one has, whether a teacher, a banker, a department store manager, or a landscaper, significantly determines what skills one possesses and cultivates, where one lives, with whom one engages, how one spends most of one's waking hours, and how much money one makes. One often has additional vocations in one's local church or community, but we should not underestimate the great dignity and potential of our professions and we should be perpetually asking how those professions become opportunities and provide resources for loving God and neighbor.[7]

Recall the way that Paul's wealth ethics took different shapes depending on whether he was itinerant or nonitinerant in a given season of his life. So also, Peter's way of life shifted significantly when he set aside itinerant ministry in order to lead the Jerusalem Church. Both of them continued to live in ways that manifested total dedication to the kingdom of God, but it was only fitting that the changes in their ways of ministering influenced the ways in which they utilized all their resources for the kingdom. So also, the place we live, the work we do, and the income we have shape the ways in which we serve the kingdom and the people to whom we can become neighbors by showing mercy.

RENOUNCING EVERYTHING

Sanctification

Nonetheless, all these comments about the need for repentance and the way our callings shape our instantiations of the imperative to renounce all possessions for the sake of the kingdom do not change one central fact: I am nowhere close to loving my neighbor as myself, and I often recoil at the idea of renouncing all my possessions! Perhaps it seems cruel to erect this impossible standard.

But this certainly should not leave us feeling miserable or hopeless, as if our sinfulness and our woundedness have become impossible barriers to holiness and wholeness. After all, the central goal of theology is to know God, and in this construal of Lukan wealth ethics, we have seen a God who is so transcendently good that he is worthy of being loved with all of our being, and a God who wants his people to be merciful as he is merciful. The fact that I am not like God does not mean that this depiction of God is bad theology. Quite the contrary, bad theology is theology that makes God into something like me.

The disparity between God's mercy and my broken selfishness should not be occasion for despair; it simply reminds me that wealth ethics, like all other areas of Christian morality, require *sanctification* for us to become the people God wants us to be. Sanctification means that God cooperates with us in making us holy. As we see in Paul's letters, sanctification is both an imperative for the believer (1 Thess 4:3) and something wrought in Christ (1 Cor 1:30) and by the Spirit (2 Thess 2:12); God helps us along in realizing his seminal command in Leviticus 20:26: "You shall be holy to me; for I the Lord am holy."

Most of us have already internalized this idea with respect to other moral issues on which Jesus teaches utterly idealistic things. Most of us don't despair when we read, "If you are angry with a brother or sister, you will be liable to judgment;...and if you say, 'You fool,' you will be liable to the hell of fire" (Matt 5:22). Instead, we recognize that Jesus is underscoring the moral gravity and the insidious, pernicious nature of hatred, and so we discipline ourselves and look to God for aid in abandoning our malice.

Likewise, recall Jesus' teachings on lust:

Guidance for the Contemporary Disciple

> You have heard that it was said, "You shall not commit adultery." But I say to you that everyone who looks at a woman with lust has already committed adultery with her in his heart. If your right eye causes you to sin, tear it out and throw it away; it is better for you to lose one of your members than for your whole body to be thrown into hell. (Matt 5:27–29)

Most readers apprehend that Jesus is using hyperbole in this passage; he does not actually want all the teenage boys in his audience to tear their eyes out. But he uses this graphic hyperbole because he wants to communicate the seriousness of prurience, so that his followers would commit themselves to greater self-control and look to God for aid in healing and transforming their desires.

So it is with wealth ethics. Luke uses graphic warnings (like the postmortem torment of Dives) and stark hyperbole (like the image of a camel passing through the eye of a needle) to communicate the enormous ethical gravity of using our wealth to love God and our neighbors. Since this was and is literally a matter of life and death for many people in the world, Luke was right to have spared no rhetorical expense. But his agenda was not merely to condemn the moral lethargy of his readers or to leave them in fatalistic despair; his agenda was to move them toward greater love, greater holiness, and greater generosity, and thereby to safeguard their souls.

Thus, as we move into repentance and reflect on our vocation, we should also move forward in sanctification, seeking healing of the wounds and traumas that impede the journey to wholeness. It is only through this process of integral restoration that we might grow to love our neighbor more and to cling to our wealth less, our will cooperating with the work of God's Spirit.

It may seem flippant to say that we ought to "love our neighbors" more, and indeed, many of our neediest neighbors live on different continents. But one practical way to begin to grow in love is simply to meet a person to whom one can become a neighbor. (As a pathological introvert, I appreciate how daunting this may feel to some readers.) But if one can overcome the fear of being asked for money or being made to feel guilty, and take the step to meet someone genuinely poor (whether in church or school or through a ministry) and get to know them, that friendship can become a catalyst for growth in love. But if our closed social circle, our suburban neighborhood, our swanky church, or our fast-moving cars (fortresses of solitude on wheels) have allowed us to isolate ourselves from the poor, then we have found a very odd way of following the Jesus who said, "When you give a luncheon or a dinner, do not invite your friends or your brothers or your relatives or rich neighbors....Invite the poor" (14:12–13).

Another practical way to cooperate with the process of sanctification is by curbing our consumption. This may need to happen just one step at a time; much like the experience of taking up exercise after years of inactivity, ambitious plans to strangle nonessential consumption often fizzle out after a couple of weeks. For me, the first step was to stop buying new books—a vice rather common among grad students—to discontinue my residency in Starbucks, and to cease visiting Blockbuster every weekend (and now I have revealed something about my age). That by no means represented success in renouncing all my possessions (!), but it was a step on the way, learning to love my little pleasures less and to free up a little more money for something more than satisfying my cravings for cappuccinos or the latest expensive monograph on global poverty.

Curbing one's consumption goes hand-in-hand with a lifetime of earnest self-reflection about the "principle of enough."[8] Whether in our domestic lives or in our professions, Christians need to develop the discipline of asking, "What is enough?" What is enough to keep me physically and emotionally well? What is enough to allow me to do my job, to realize my vocation, with diligence? What is a sufficient investment in my child's education, so that she can realize her own calling? What are sufficiently reasonable precautions for my family's safety and security? This "principle of enough" will help us undermine consumptive patterns that are consequences of mere habit or our social context, so that we can spend less on superfluous things and more on the love of God and neighbor. And indeed, growth in love of our neighbor (as well as knowledge of our poor neighbor's life) will likely transform our definition of what is enough.

These steps are beginnings. They do not represent faithful renunciation of all possessions nor total commitment to God nor loving one's neighbor as oneself. But they do represent progress in sanctification, our cooperation with God's work of creating us to be what we are, work that will only be complete when the kingdom of this world has become the kingdom of our God and of his Christ (Rev 11:15). The notion that God will cooperate with us in our discipleship should be simultaneously comforting and daunting: comforting because "the one who began a good work among you will bring it to completion by the day of Jesus Christ" (Phil 1:6); and daunting because it's a long road to perfect love, perfect holiness, and perfect mercy. Our cooperation with the divine Helper in sanctification is captured in the effortless prose of C. S. Lewis:

> This Helper who will, in the long run, be satisfied with nothing less than absolute perfection, will also be delighted with the first feeble, stumbling effort you make tomorrow to do the simplest duty....Every father is pleased with a baby's first attempt to walk: [but] no father would be satisfied with anything less than a firm, free manly walk in a grown-up son....
>
> The practical upshot is this. On the one hand, God's demand for perfection need not discourage you in the least in your present attempts to be good, or even in your present failures. Each time you fall He will pick you up again. And He knows perfectly well that your own efforts are never going to bring you anywhere near perfection. On the other hand, you must realise from the outset that the goal towards which He is beginning to guide you is absolute perfection, and no power in the universe, except you yourself, can prevent Him from taking you to that goal. That is what you are in for.[9]

So, as Paul says, "Whenever we have an opportunity, let us work for the good of all, and especially for those of the family of faith" (Gal 6:10).

Notes

Acknowledgments

1. *Luke's Wealth Ethics: A Study in Their Coherence and Character*, Wissenschaftliche Untersuchungen zum Neuen Testament II, vol. 275 (Tübingen: Mohr Siebeck, 2010).

Chapter 1

1. Luke Timothy Johnson, *The Literary Function of Possessions in Luke-Acts*, SBL Dissertation Series 39 (Missoula, MT: Scholars, 1977), 233.

2. The reader may notice that the book alternates between talking about Luke, Luke's Jesus, and Jesus. This is not to drive a wedge between Luke and Jesus; rather, it owes to the fact that sometimes Luke is doing things with his Jesus traditions that Mark and Matthew are not doing. I do not mean to imply that Luke has misrepresented Jesus (in fact, the present author tends to think that Luke is quite historically careful). Nonetheless, it is entirely appropriate to focus on Luke as an author and as a Gospel, based on the conviction that Luke's Gospel is Scripture, even in details that cannot be reliably ascribed to the historical Jesus.

3. Cf. Philip, the Evangelist: Acts 21:8; Simon, the Tanner: Acts 9:43; Cornelius: Acts 10:48; Mary, the mother of John: Acts 12:13; and Lydia: Acts 10:15, 40.

4. So also: "All who believed were together and had all things in common; they would sell their possessions and goods and distribute the proceeds to all, as any had need" (Acts 2:44–45).

5. Karl Kautsky, *The Foundations of Early Christianity: A Study in Christian Origins* (London: Orbach and Chambers, 1925), 331–47.

6. This is not to imply that anyone is truly objective (the history of modern philosophy has revealed pure objectivity to be a bit of a pipe dream), but there are lots of ways that one can be *more* or *less* objective.

7. Indeed, the vast majority of New Testament scholars are themselves committed Christians who chose their professions for the same reason that laypeople read the Bible devotionally: they want to know God.

8. Student readers should understand that each of the positions described here is defended in far more detail than can be done justice in a space sufficiently brief to keep their attention! So, in fairness to the scholars who have actually elaborated their views in great detail (and mostly in German), I have chosen to discuss the basic themes in abstract, without referencing any one figure in particular. For a properly nuanced description and critique of multiple proponents of each explanation, see *LWE*, 3–20.

9. See chapter 6 on the "theo-logic" of Luke's wealth ethics.

10. The "Ebionites" were an early Jewish-Christian sect that valued voluntary poverty.

11. When scholars talk about "wandering charismatic radicals," they refer to itinerant preachers who worked miracles and tended to practice a sort of ascetic simplicity.

12. For a summary of the historical Jesus evidence, see Christopher M. Hays, "Rich & Poor," in *Dictionary of Jesus and the Gospels*, ed. Joel B. Green, Jeannine K. Brown, and Nicholas Perrin (Downers Grove, IL: IVP Academic, 2013), 802–4.

13. The earliest proponent of this view argued that the term *disciple* actually denotes only the Twelve and the Seventy, and not the rest of Jesus' followers (Hans-Joachim Degenhardt, *Lukas, Evangelist der Armen: Besitz und Besitzverzicht in den lukanischen Schriften: eine traditions- und redaktionsgeschichtliche Untersuchung* [Stuttgart: Katholisches Bibelwerk, 1965], 31, 39) but that suggestion has been roundly rejected. See David Peter Seccombe, *Possessions and the Poor in Luke-Acts*, Studien zum Neuen Testament und seiner Umwelt, series B, vol. 6 (Linz: A. Fuchs, 1982), 101–5; *LWE*, 3–4.

Notes

14. See chapter 4.
15. See chapter 3.

Chapter 2

1. The scholarly book that was key in bringing about this consensus is Richard A. Burridge, *What Are the Gospels? A Comparison with Graeco-Roman Biography*, 2nd ed. (Grand Rapids: Eerdmans Press, 2004).

2. On legumes, see Diogenes Laertius, *Lives of Eminent Philosophers* 8.39–40; Iamblicus, *Vita Pyth.* 61; on justice and communalism, see Diogenes Laertius, *Lives of Eminent Philosophers* 8.10; 10.11; Iamblicus, *Vita Pyth.* 167–68.

3. Xenophon, Ages. 10.2; Isocrates, Evag. 73–78; Philo, *Abr.* 3-5; Lucian, *Demon.* 2.

4. As opposed to just describing the ethics of Jesus' earthly ministry as a matter of historical interest, which is the tactic taken by advocates of the interim explanation of Lukan wealth ethics; see chapter 1.

5. In this context, *propositional* means "stated in direct terms," as opposed to being illustrated by example or suggested implicitly (which are the ways in which narratives typically teach ethics). For example, a propositional statement on the deity of Christ would be "Jesus is God, the incarnate Logos," whereas a narrative affirmation of the same idea would show Jesus doing God-like things, such as calming a stormy sea or forgiving sins. Similarly, a propositional teaching about wealth ethics might be "Christians should feed the hungry," while a narrative teaching to the same effect would show apostles (the heroes of Acts) feeding needy believers in their own homes (thus Acts 2:42), while a selfish rich man is punished with suffering because he does not share his banquets with a hungry beggar (thus Luke 16:19–31).

6. Gordon D. Fee and Douglas Stuart, *How to Read the Bible for All It's Worth*, 4th ed. (Grand Rapids: Zondervan, 2014), 73.

7. For more detailed explanations of exemplary or paradigmatic figures in Luke and Acts, see William S. Kurz, "Narrative Models for Imitation in Luke-Acts," in *Greeks, Romans, and Christians: Essays in Honor of Abraham J. Malherbe*, ed. David L. Balch (Minneapolis: Fortress Press, 1990), 171–89; Kari Syreeni,

"The Gospel in Paradigms: A Study in the Hermeneutical Space of Luke-Acts," in *Luke-Acts: Scandinavian Perspectives*, ed. Petri Luomanen, *Publications of the Finnish Exegetical Society* 54 (Göttingen: Vandenhoeck & Ruprecht, 1991), 36–57.

8. One of the biggest bridges between the ancient narrative and the contemporary world is the belief that the God of the ancient narrative is the same God who is worshipped by the Church today, that God has not changed and that God's commitment to his people is the same (Mal 3:6; Heb 13:8). That continuity of divine character does not mean that one slavishly reenacts the practices of the ancient people of God, but that one imitates them as is appropriate for people in relationship to the same God, albeit in a very different set of circumstances.

9. For example, Mark's version of Jesus' interaction with the rich young ruler says, "Jesus, looking at him, loved him" (Mark 10:21). Luke, however, drops this phrase entirely (note Luke 18:22) and launches straight into the imperative to sell all his possessions and give the money to the poor. Luke omits the comment about Jesus' love for the rich man in order to sharpen the reader's apprehension of the seriousness of the command to sell all and to increase the poignancy of Jesus' warning about the dangers of wealth.

Chapter 3

1. *Tg., Onq., Neof.,* and *Ps.-Jon.* Deut 6:5; *m. Ber.* 9:55//*b. Ber.* 54a.

2. Matthew would have agreed with the point, as one can see in Matthew 25:34–45, where Jesus rejects people who call him "Lord" because they did not serve his most-insignificant brethren.

3. Richard Bauckham, "The Scrupulous Priest and the Good Samaritan: Jesus' Parabolic Interpretation of the Law of Moses," *New Testament Studies* 44 (1998): 475–89; J. Duncan M. Derrett, "Law in the New Testament: Fresh Light on the Parable of the Good Samaritan," *New Testament Studies* 10 (1964): 22–37.

4. For detail on this, see Christopher M. Hays, "Hating Wealth and Wives? An Examination of Discipleship Ethics in the Third Gospel," *Tyndale Bulletin* 60, no. 1 (2009): 54–56. Obviously, there is some *prima facie* tension between the idea that you

are supposed to hate your family and yet love your neighbor as yourself. This tension is somewhat resolved, however, by noting that the double love command does prioritize love of God over love of neighbor: one loves God more than oneself, dedicating all that one is to God, but one is to love one's neighbor only *as* oneself, thus, less than God. Therefore, in the event that one's commitment of God comes into conflict with one's commitment to one's life, one's neighbor, or one's family, the commitment to God takes precedence, even if that makes it look as though one hates one's family.

5. See, for example, Matt 3:5; 4:24; 21:26; 23:5; Mark 1:5, 37; 7:3; Luke 5:17; 20:45; 21:17, 38; 22:70; Acts 1:1, 19; 9:35; 18:17; 19:10, 17; 21:28; 26:4.

6. Similarly, John 21:25 says—also hyperbolically—"There are also many other things that Jesus did; if every one of them were written down, I suppose that the world itself could not contain the books that would be written."

7. For example, when I tell my students, "It is essential that you read the syllabus carefully," I am using hyperbole. Knowing every detail in my syllabus may not be *absolutely necessary* for a student to succeed in my class, but it will be an important factor in whether the student gets the grade hoped for.

8. Eusebius, *Hist. eccl.* 2.17.5; Philo, *Migr.* 92; P.Oxy. 904.8 (quitting a civic office); Iamblichus, *Vita Pyth.* 13 (desisting from certain practices).

Chapter 4

1. Yes, this is the group from which we get the word *cynical*, but that doesn't mean the philosophy was just jaded and pessimistic.

2. See, for example, Diogenes Laertius 6.13, 104; Dio Chrysostom 6:14–15, 30–31; Diogenes, *Ep.* 7.1, 15, 19; 30.3–4. For a great introduction to Cynicism, see F. Gerald Downing, *Cynics and Christian Origins* (Edinburgh: T&T Clark, 1992).

3. See, for example, Josephus, *A.J.* 18.21; *B.J.* 2.119–27; Philo, *Prob.* 85–87; CD 14.14–17; 1QS 6.16–25; for an excellent discussion of the Essenes, see Brian J. Capper, "Essene Community Houses and Jesus' Early Community," in *Jesus and Archaeology*,

ed. James H. Charlesworth (Grand Rapids, MI: Eerdmans, 2006), 472–98.

4. Some scholars have argued that Jesus and the Twelve actually *were* Cynic or Essene preachers, but that probably overstates the similarities between the groups. See *LWE*, 91–93.

5. It is very widely agreed that the Gospel of Mark was one of Luke's sources. It is less common to think that Luke used Matthew's Gospel; the majority of scholars would say that Luke and Matthew both used a source that is now lost to us, which scholars just call "Q." The present author, however, is skeptical that Q existed. For an account of why an increasing number of academics think Luke used Matthew instead of Q, see Mark Goodacre, *The Synoptic Problem: A Way through the Maze* (London: Sheffield Academic, 2001).

6. See chapter 3.

7. See Luise Schottroff and Wolfgang Stegemann, *Jesus and the Hope of the Poor*, trans. Matthew J. O'Connell (Maryknoll, NY: Orbis Books, 1986), 7–9.

8. Note that Luke 9:58 occurs right between these two sets of instructions for itinerant ministry.

9. Though if you are curious, see *LWE*, 93–100.

10. There has been some fascinating speculation that Mary and Joanna were merchant women who connected through business interests before meeting Jesus; see Marianne Sawicki, "Magdalenes and Tiberiennes: City Women in the Entourage of Jesus," in *Transformative Encounters: Jesus and the Women Re-Viewed*, ed. Ingrid Rosa Kitzberger, Biblical Interpretation 43 (Leiden: Brill, 2000), 181–202.

11. This is at least clear in the parallel versions in Mark 10:22 and Matt 19:22; Luke 18:23 only narrates how Jesus' teachings sorrowed the man, and leaves under-defined whether the man actually walks away.

12. Schottroff and Stegemann, *Jesus and the Hope of the Poor*, 8–9.

13. The fourfold restitution Zacchaeus proposes is probably not a function of obeying Old Testament laws about theft, which generally required the return of what was taken plus 20 percent (Lev 6:2–5). More likely, Zacchaeus is conforming to Roman legal conventions that required fourfold restitution; see Justinian, *Dig.*

Notes

39.4; A. J. Kerr, "Zacchaeus's Decision to Make Fourfold Restitution," *Expository Times* 98, no. 3 (1986–87): 70. Picking this more rigorous penalty for malfeasance underscores the earnestness of Zacchaeus's intention to make up for his injustice.

14. This is to say that she had already entirely committed her care to the God who feeds the birds and clothes the lilies of the field (12:24–31); see chapter 6.

Chapter 5

1. Some of the best examples of this approach are Robert C. Tannehill, *The Narrative Unity of Luke-Acts: A Literary Interpretation: Volume 1: The Gospel of Luke* (Philadelphia: Fortress Press, 1986); *The Narrative Unity of Luke-Acts: A Literary Interpretation: Volume 2: The Acts of the Apostles* (Minneapolis: Fortress Press, 1994).

2. Canon lists are just lists of all the New Testament books in order.

3. The best recent survey of the debate can be found in C. Kavin Rowe and Andrew Gregory, eds., *Rethinking the Unity and Reception of Luke and Acts* (Columbia, SC: University of South Carolina Press, 2010).

4. Diodorus Siculus, 17.118.4; Richard A. Burridge, *What Are the Gospels? A Comparison with Graeco-Roman Biography*, 2nd ed. (Grand Rapids, MI: Eerdmans, 2004), 239.

5. Especially explaining the extension of God's mission to Gentiles who do not adopt Jewish circumcision and purity laws.

6. On Acts as historiography, see Ben Witherington, *The Acts of the Apostles: A Socio-Rhetorical Commentary* (Grand Rapids, MI: Eerdmans, 1998), 17–21.

7. See Colin J. Hemer, *The Book of Acts in the Setting of Hellenistic Historiography*, Wissenschaftliche Untersuchungen zum Neuen Testament 49 (Tübingen: J.C.B. Mohr [Paul Siebeck], 1989), 80–82.

8. Defending, for example, Christian nonobservance of Jewish food laws and fraternization with Gentiles (see Acts 9:51—11:18).

9. CD 13.9–10; 1QS 7.6–25; Josephus, *Ant.* 18.21; *B.J.* 2.119–23; Philo, *Prob.* 85–87.

10. The most compelling advocate of this position is Brian J. Capper. His essays include "The Palestinian Cultural Context of the Earliest Christian Community of Goods," in *The Book of Acts in Its Palestinian Setting*, ed. Richard Bauckham, The Book of Acts in its First Century Setting 4 (Grand Rapids, MI: Eerdmans, 1995), 323–56; "Essene Community Houses and Jesus' Early Community," in *Jesus and Archaeology*, ed. James H. Charlesworth (Grand Rapids, MI: Eerdmans, 2006), 472–502. Capper's work is fascinating, and while his understanding of the Essenes themselves is quite convincing, I have expressed my disagreements with his analysis of Acts in *LWE*, 195–209, 216–22, 228–32.

11. See Diogenes Laertius 8.10; 10.11; Iamblichus, *Vita Pyth.* 32, 92.

12. Plato, *Resp.* 424A; 449C; *Leg.* 739C.

13. Iamblichus, *Vita Pyth.* 30, 32, 81, 167–68; Plato, *Resp.* 416D–E; 423E–424A; 449C; 457C–D; 464A–D; 543B–C; *Tim.* 18B–D.

14. See, for example, Aristotle, *Eth. nic.* 8.9.1, 1159b31–32; Cicero, *Off.* 1.51; Seneca, *Ben.* 7.4.1.

15. Aristotle, *Pol.* 2.2.5, 1263a34–39.

16. Aristotle, *Eth. nic.* 9.8.2, 1168b8; Diogenes Laertius 5.20.

17. Luke's purpose in these texts is not to give a full-orbed theology of salvation and damnation, but to push his readers toward generosity. While one should not blithely discard Luke's teachings about the connection between wealth ethics and one's eternal state, one should also be careful not to reduce the dynamics of salvation to greed and generosity.

18. In Luke, being "outside" means being excluded from the kingdom of God and banished to a place of weeping and gnashing of teeth (13:25, 28; cf. 14:15, 24).

19. The phrase "it is more blessed to give than to receive" in 20:35 is called an *agraphon*, a saying of Jesus that is not recorded in any of the canonical Gospels. There is, however, little reason to doubt that it is a genuine Jesus tradition, since it fits neatly with Jesus' many teachings about money and generosity.

Notes

Chapter 6

1. For example, if you believe in the existence of hell (which is a theological commitment, not a philosophical one) and if you believe that God will send people to hell for neglecting the poor (Matt 25:31–46), then it is logical to argue that you should care for the needy in order to avoid going to hell. If, however, you don't believe in hell, or you don't believe that your eternal state is affected by whether or not you help hungry people, then you won't find the logic of Matthew 25:31–46 to be very compelling, and you will not choose to care for the poor for that reason (even though you may decide to care for the poor on the basis of *other* reasons).

2. Luke 12:30; Gen 2:20–22; 1 Tim 6:8; Sir 29:21.

3. For the details of the grammar behind this translation, see *LWE*, 120–21.

4. For a survey of the Old Testament teachings on justice and care for the poor, see Craig Blomberg, *Neither Poverty nor Riches: A Biblical Theology of Material Possessions*, New Studies in Biblical Theology (Grand Rapids, MI: Eerdmans, 1999), 33–86; John R. Donahue, *Seek Justice That You May Live: Reflections and Resources on the Bible and Social Justice* (New York: Paulist Press, 2014); *LWE*, 28–45.

5. The idea that almsgiving can forgive sins seems very strange to Protestant readers, but it was a strongly held belief of ancient Jews and the early Christians; for a detailed treatment of the topic, see David J. Downs, *Alms: Charity, Reward, and Atonement in Early Christianity* (Waco, TX: Baylor University Press, 2016); Gary A. Anderson, "Redeem Your Sins by the Giving of Alms: Sin, Debt, and the "Treasury of Merit" in Jewish and Early Christian Tradition," *Letter and Spirit* 3 (2007): 37–67.

6. Likewise, when Jesus responds to the rich ruler's claim to have kept the commandments since his youth (18:20–21), he says that one thing remains for the man to do: give his goods to the poor (18:22). This implies that the one command the rich ruler has failed to keep is the command to practice charity.

7. Prov 8:21; 10:4; 12:27; 13:4, 18, 21; 20:4, 13.

8. Classic reversal texts in the Old Testament include 1 Sam 2:7; Isa 26:5–6; Zeph 3:11–12; Sir 11:5, 13, 21. The motif continues

to be developed in extrabiblical Jewish literature: *T. Jud.* 2.4; *1En.* 103.3–15; *Sib. Or.* 3.350–355; 4Q171 2.9–12; 4Q427 7.2.7–11.

9. For greater detail, see John O. York, *The Last Shall Be First: The Rhetoric of Reversal in Luke,* Journal for the Study of the New Testament Supplement Series 46 (Worcester, UK: JSOT Press, 1991).

10. Exod 22:25–27; Deut 10:17–19; Pss 10:17–18; 12:5; 35:10; 68:5; 72:4, 12–13; 146:7–10; Isa 3:14–15; 25:4; Amos 8:4–7.

11. To unpack why these interactions make sense within a first-century honor/shame society, see David T. Landry and Ben May, "Honor Restored: New Light on the Parable of the Prudent Steward (Luke 16:1–8a)," *Journal of Biblical Literature* 119, no. 2 (2000): 287–309; *LWE,* 140–44.

12. A similar dynamic is present in the parable of the vine and the elm in the early second-century text *The Shepherd of Hermas*; see Herm. *Sim.* 2:1–10.

Chapter 7

1. Compare the formulation of Catholic ethicist Germain Grisez: "All Jesus' followers must give up everything they have, in the sense of investing all their material goods in God's kingdom.... To devote material goods to the service of Jesus' kingdom means acquiring, using, and retaining them precisely insofar as they are necessary for survival or are suitable for fulfilling responsibilities pertaining to one's personal vocation." Germain Grisez, *The Way of the Lord Jesus: Volume Two: Living a Christian Life* (Quincy, IL: Franciscan Herald, 1993), 804.

2. At the risk of stating the obvious, Luke does not think that renouncing possessions entails that one deprives oneself of what one needs for one's own survival. After all, Paul makes tents, not only to help the needy, but also to care for his own needs (Acts 20:34–35)!

3. The first tithe, that is, but not the second tithe, which was to be given to the poor once every three years; cf. Lev 27:30–33; Num 18:21–24; Deut 14:22–27.

4. Although there were ancient alimentary foundations that did something similar to the scenario described here as an

alternative to the divestiture practiced by Barnabas, Ananias, and Sapphira. Especially in Italy in the first and second centuries, rich people *would* designate that a piece of property be worked in perpetuity and that the proceeds be given to support orphans!

5. Check out their website, https://www.givingwhatwecan.org/.

6. Toby Ord, "The Moral Imperative towards Cost-Effectiveness in Global Health," (Center for Global Development, 2013), published March 11, 2013, http://www.cgdev.org/publication/moral-imperative-toward-cost-effectiveness-global-health.

7. For a more fulsome discussion of this point, see Kenman L. Wong and Scott B. Rae, *Business for the Common Good: A Christian Vision for the Marketplace*, Christian Worldview Integration Series (Downers Grove, IL: IVP Academic, 2011), 39–91.

8. William E. Diehl, "The Guided Market System," in *Wealth and Poverty: Four Christian Views of Economics*, ed. Robert G. Clouse (Downers Grove, IL: InterVarsity, 1984), 106.

9. C. S. Lewis, *Mere Christianity* (New York: Simon & Schuster, 1943, 1996), 174.

Bibliography

Anderson, Gary A. "Redeem Your Sins by the Giving of Alms: Sin, Debt, and the 'Treasury of Merit' in Jewish and Early Christian Tradition." *Letter and Spirit* 3 (2007): 37–67.

Bauckham, Richard. "The Scrupulous Priest and the Good Samaritan: Jesus' Parabolic Interpretation of the Law of Moses." *New Testament Studies* 44 (1998): 475–89.

Blomberg, Craig. *Neither Poverty nor Riches: A Biblical Theology of Material Possessions*. New Studies in Biblical Theology. Grand Rapids: Eerdmans, 1999.

Burridge, Richard A. *What Are the Gospels? A Comparison with Graeco-Roman Biography*. 2nd ed. Grand Rapids: Eerdmans, 2004.

Capper, Brian J. "Essene Community Houses and Jesus' Early Community." In *Jesus and Archaeology*, edited by James H. Charlesworth, 472–502. Grand Rapids: Eerdmans, 2006.

———. "The Palestinian Cultural Context of the Earliest Christian Community of Goods." In *The Book of Acts in Its Palestinian Setting*, edited by Richard Bauckham, 323–56. The Book of Acts in Its First Century Setting, vol. 4. Grand Rapids: Eerdmans, 1995.

Degenhardt, Hans-Joachim. *Lukas, Evangelist der Armen: Besitz und Besitzverzicht in den lukanischen Schriften: eine traditions- und redaktionsgeschichtliche Untersuchung*. Stuttgart: Katholisches Bibelwerk, 1965.

Derrett, J. Duncan M. "Law in the New Testament: Fresh Light on the Parable of the Good Samaritan." *New Testament Studies* 10 (1964): 22–37.

Diehl, William E. "The Guided Market System." In *Wealth and Poverty: Four Christian Views of Economics*, edited by Robert G. Clouse. Downers Grove, IL: InterVarsity, 1984.

Donahue, John R. *Seek Justice That You May Live: Reflections and Resources on the Bible and Social Justice*. New York: Paulist Press, 2014.

Downing, F. Gerald. *Cynics and Christian Origins*. Edinburgh: T&T Clark, 1992.

Downs, David J. *Alms: Charity, Reward, and Atonement in Early Christianity*. Waco, TX: Baylor University Press, 2016.

Fee, Gordon D., and Douglas Stuart. *How to Read the Bible for All It's Worth*. 4th ed. Grand Rapids: Zondervan, 2014.

Goodacre, Mark. *The Synoptic Problem: A Way through the Maze*. London: Sheffield Academic, 2001.

Grisez, Germain. *The Way of the Lord Jesus: Volume Two: Living a Christian Life*. Quincy, IL: Franciscan Herald, 1993.

Hays, Christopher M. "Hating Wealth and Wives? An Examination of Discipleship Ethics in the Third Gospel." *Tyndale Bulletin* 60, no. 1 (2009): 47–68.

———. *Luke's Wealth Ethics: A Study in Their Coherence and Character*. Wissenschaftliche Untersuchungen zum Neuen Testament II, vol. 275. Tübingen: Mohr Siebeck, 2010.

———. "Rich & Poor." In *Dictionary of Jesus and the Gospels*, edited by Joel B. Green, Jeannine K. Brown, and Nicholas Perrin, 800–10. Downers Grove, IL: IVP Academic, 2013.

Hemer, Colin J. *The Book of Acts in the Setting of Hellenistic Historiography*. Wissenschaftliche Untersuchungen zum Neuen Testament, vol. 49. Tübingen: J.C.B. Mohr (Paul Siebeck), 1989.

Johnson, Luke Timothy. *The Literary Function of Possessions in Luke-Acts*. SBL Dissertation Series, vol. 39. Missoula, MT: Scholars, 1977.

Kautsky, Karl. *The Foundations of Early Christianity: A Study in Christian Origins*. London: Orbach and Chambers, 1925.

Kerr, A. J. "Zacchaeus's Decision to Make Fourfold Restitution." *Expository Times* 98, no. 3 (1986–87): 68–71.

Kurz, William S. "Narrative Models for Imitation in Luke-Acts." In *Greeks, Romans, and Christians: Essays in Honor of*

Bibliography

Abraham J. Malherbe, edited by David L. Balch, 171–89. Minneapolis: Fortress, 1990.

Landry, David T., and Ben May. "Honor Restored: New Light on the Parable of the Prudent Steward (Luke 16:1–8a)." *Journal of Biblical Literature* 119, no. 2 (2000): 287–309.

Lewis, C. S. *Mere Christianity*. New York: Simon & Schuster, 1943, 1996.

Ord, Toby. "The Moral Imperative towards Cost-Effectiveness in Global Health." Center for Global Development, March 11, 2013. http://www.cgdev.org/publication/moral-imperative-toward-cost-effectiveness-global-health.

Rowe, C. Kavin, and Andrew Gregory, eds. *Rethinking the Unity and Reception of Luke and Acts*. Columbia, SC: University of South Carolina Press, 2010.

Sawicki, Marianne. "Magdalenes and Tiberiennes: City Women in the Entourage of Jesus." In *Transformative Encounters: Jesus and the Women Re-Viewed*, edited by Ingrid Rosa Kitzberger, 181–202. Biblical Interpretation, vol. 43. Leiden: Brill, 2000.

Schottroff, Luise, and Wolfgang Stegemann. *Jesus and the Hope of the Poor*. Translated by Matthew J. O'Connell. Maryknoll, NY: Orbis, 1986.

Seccombe, David Peter. *Possessions and the Poor in Luke-Acts*. SNTU series B, vol. 6. Linz: A. Fuchs, 1982.

Syreeni, Kari. "The Gospel in Paradigms: A Study in the Hermeneutical Space of Luke-Acts." In *Luke-Acts: Scandinavian Perspectives*, edited by Petri Luomanen, 36–57. Publications of the Finnish Exegetical Society, vol. 54. Göttingen: Vandenhoeck & Ruprecht, 1991.

Tannehill, Robert C. *The Narrative Unity of Luke-Acts: A Literary Interpretation: Volume 1: The Gospel of Luke*. Philadelphia: Fortress, 1986.

———. *The Narrative Unity of Luke-Acts: A Literary Interpretation: Volume 2: The Acts of the Apostles*. Minneapolis: Fortress, 1994.

Witherington, Ben. *The Acts of the Apostles: A Socio-Rhetorical Commentary*. Grand Rapids: Eerdmans, 1998.

Wong, Kenman L., and Scott B. Rae. *Business for the Common Good: A Christian Vision for the Marketplace*. Christian

Worldview Integration Series. Downers Grove, IL: IVP Academic, 2011.

York, John O. *The Last Shall Be First: The Rhetoric of Reversal in Luke.* Journal for the Study of the New Testament Supplement Series, vol. 46. Worcester, UK: JSOT Press, 1991.

Index of Sources

OLD TESTAMENT

Genesis
2:20–22	105n2

Exodus
22:25–27	106n10

Leviticus
6:2–5	102n13
19	28
19:11–17	28
19:18	26, 28, 69, 71
20:26	92
27:30–33	106n3

Numbers
18:21–24	106n3

Deuteronomy
6:5	26, 69
10:17–19	106n10
14:22–27	106n3
15:4–5	57

1 Samuel
2:7	105n8

Job
38:22	16

Psalms
10:17–18	106n10
12:5	106n10
35:10	106n10
68:5	106n10
72:4	106n10
72:12–13	106n10
146:7–10	106n10

Proverbs
8:21	105n7
10:4	105n7
12:27	105n7
13:4	105n7
13:18	105n7
13:21	105n7
15:27	71
19:17	77
20:4	105n7
20:13	105n7

Ecclesiastes
2:20	33

Isaiah
3:14–15	106n10
25:4	106n10
26:5–6	105n8
58:6–7	70, 71
61:1	71
61:1–3	70

Daniel
4:27	71

Amos
8:4–7	106n10

Micah
6:8	71

Zephaniah
3:11–12	105n8

Malachi
3:6	100n8

NEW TESTAMENT

Matthew
3:5	101n5
4:18–22	38
4:22	38
4:24	101n5
5:22	92
5:27–29	93
5:48	29
6:33	74
13:22	10
19:21	10
19:22	102n11
19:23–26	10
21:26	101n5
22:36	26
22:39	26
22:40	26
23:5	101n5
25:31–46	62, 105n1
25:34–45	100n2

Mark
1:5	101n5
1:16–20	38
1:20	38
1:37	101n5
2:14	39
4:19	10
7:3	101n5
10:21	44, 100n9
10:22	102n11
10:23–27	10
10:29–30	44
12:31	26

Luke
1:1–3	23
1:1–4	23
1:20–22	61
3:3	89
3:4	88
3:7	89
3:8	89
3:9	89
3:10	89
3:11	4, 86
3:11–14	89
4	43
4:18	71, 78
4:18–19	70, 79
4:21	70
4:28–29	20

Index of Sources

4:38–39	37	9:23	8
5:1–10	38	9:23–24	20
5:11	8, 11, 38, 74	9:27	8
5:17	101n5	9:51	7
5:27	11, 39	9:51—19:28	8
5:27–32	45	9:57–58	36
5:28	8, 39, 74	9:58	102
5:29	37, 39	9:62	1, 43
5:31–32	90	10	41, 50, 60, 62, 69
6:17–20	20	10:1–11	3, 11, 40, 74, 79
6:20	1, 3, 8, 73, 76, 78	10:3	40, 41, 75
6:20–23	78	10:4	3, 40, 41
6:23	90	10:5	4
6:24	1, 9, 73, 76	10:5–9	3, 11, 40, 49
6:29–35	69	10:5–11	49
6:30–31	90	10:9	4
6:31	27	10:27	26, 31, 43, 46, 63, 68, 71, 79, 82, 88
6:32–35	76		
6:33–34	90	10:28	44
6:35	69	10:29	28
6:35–36	91	10:30–35	28
6:36	29, 69	10:30–37	69
6:37	91	10:36–37	28
6:38	90	10:37	29
7:22	78	10:38–40	37
7:36–50	90	11:37–38	37
7:37	42	11:37–42	79, 86
7:47	90	11:37–52	70
8	12	11:39	63
8:1–3	37, 42, 48	11:39–42	70
8:1–13	83	11:41	2, 71
8:2	90	11:42	71, 84
8:3	12, 90	12	75
8:7	72	12:15	63
8:14	10, 43, 63, 72, 79	12:15–21	86
9	41, 50, 60, 62	12:16–20	73
9:1–6	11, 40, 74, 79	12:16–21	43, 61
9:3	40, 41	12:22	74
9:4	40, 48, 49	12:22–28	40

115

12:22–31	79	15:1	90
12:23	74	15:11–32	90
12:24	74	16:1–4	78
12:24–31	103n14	16:1–8a	106n11
12:27–30	74	16:1–9	78, 79
12:30	105n2	16:5–7	78
12:31	74, 82	16:5–8	78
12:33	1, 3, 9, 57, 60	16:9	78
12:34	1, 82	16:11–12	78
13:25	13, 104n18	16:13	62, 63, 65
13:28	13, 104n18	16:19–26	9
14:1–24	37, 76	16:19–31	62, 71, 73, 76, 79, 99
14:8–11	76		
14:12	76	16:25	76, 79
14:12–13	94	16:29	71
14:13	76	16:29–30	79
14:13–34	1	16:31	71
14:14	77, 78, 79	18	60
14:15	77, 104n18	18:18	3, 43, 44
14:15–24	73	18:18–30	39, 45, 83
14:16–24	79	18:20	43
14:21	77	18:20–21	105n6
14:21–24	78	18:21	51
14:24	77, 78, 104n18	18:22	3, 10, 43, 74, 79, 100n9, 105n6
14:25	30		
14:25–26	30, 31	18:22–25	44
14:25–33	30, 31	18:23	11, 102n11
14:26	30	18:23–24	3
14:26–27	83	18:24–25	72, 79
14:27	7, 8	18:24–27	10
14:28–33	43	18:27	73
14:33	3, 11, 12, 13, 30, 31, 32, 33, 35, 38, 39, 40, 43, 44, 46, 50, 51, 60, 61, 62, 63, 65, 69, 75, 79, 82, 85	19:1–10	11, 73, 83
		19:2	45
		19:5–6	37
		19:7	46
		19:8	4, 46
		19:9	4, 47
14:34–35	13, 62	19:28	7
14:35	65	20	85

Index of Sources

20:35	104n19	2:46	57, 59
20:45	101n5	3:6	60
21:1–4	48, 82, 83	4	59, 85
21:2	48	4:30–35	56
21:3–4	48	4:32	4, 56, 57, 58, 59
21:17	101n5	4:32–35	83
21:38	32, 101n5	4:33–35	56, 58
22	41	4:33–37	65
22:5	61	4:34	4, 21, 57
22:7–13	37	4:34–35	58
22:25	91	4:34–37	8
22:25–26	20	4:35	58, 68
22:27	20	4:36–37	60
22:33–35	83	4:37	21, 58
22:35	75	5:1	58
22:35–36	12	5:1–2	60
22:35–38	40, 41, 45	5:1–11	21, 65
22:36	40	5:2	58
22:38	41	5:3	61
22:70	101n5	5:3–4	61
23:49	42	5:5	61
23:50–53	73	5:8–10	61
24:10	42	8:9–24	63
		9:8–9	61
John		9:35	101n5
13:14–15	21	9:36	2
21:25	101n6	9:36–41	63
		9:43	63, 97n3
Acts		9:51—11:18	103n8
1:1	101n5	10:2	2
1:16–20	61	10:2–6	63
1:19	101n5	10:15	97n3
2	59, 85	10:31–32	63
2:42	99n5	10:32	63
2:42–47	56, 83	10:40	97n3
2:44	58	10:48	63, 97n3
2:44–45	56, 58, 97n4	11:27–30	63, 65
2:44–46	58	12	19
2:45	58, 68	12:13	97n3

12:23	61	**2 Corinthians**	
13:11	61	11:8–9	62
16:5	63		
16:14	42	**Galatians**	
16:15	62	6:10	95
16:16–19	63		
17:5–6	63	**Philippians**	
17:18	58	1:6	95
18:2–3	62, 63	4:10–11	62
18:3	12		
18:17	101n5	**1 Thessalonians**	
19:9	62	2:9	62
19:10	101n5	4:3	92
19:17	101n5		
19:25–27	63	**2 Thessalonians**	
20:34	21, 63	2:12	92
20:34–35	12, 65, 83, 106n2		
20:35	21, 32, 62, 63	**1 Timothy**	
21:8	97n3	6:8	105n2
21:8–10	62, 63	6:18–19	71
21:16	62, 63		
21:28	101n5	**Hebrews**	
24:25–26	64	13:8	100n8
26:4	101n5		
		Revelation	
Romans		11:15	95
1:52–53	75		
2:34	75	**DEUTEROCANONICAL BOOKS**	
3:7–14	75		
12—15	25	**Sirach**	
12:1–2	25	3:30	71
		11:5	105n8
1 Corinthians		11:13	105n8
1:30	92	11:21	105n8
4:12	62	29:21	105n2
9:4–12	62		
12:4–31	85